YONDER GROUND

A VILLAGE HISTORY

Anthony Blad

First published in 1993 by Anthony Blad
Bridles Cottage, Bloxworth, Wareham, Dorset

Copyright © Anthony Blad 1993

ISBN 0 9522581 0 2

British Library Cataloguing in Publication Data
A CIP record for this book is available
from the British Library

Main Sources of Information

The Public Record Office
The Dorset County Record Office
The Dorset County Museum
The Wiltshire County Record Office
Hutchins *History of Dorset*

Typeset by M.E. King, St Andrews Road, Bridport, Dorset
Printed by Sherrens the Printers, South Park, Avon Close,
Granby Industrial Estate, Weymouth DT4 9YX

CONTENTS

List of Maps and Illustrations		ii
Preface		1
Introduction		2
Chapter 1	The Sixteenth Century - In Tudor Times (1539-1603)	3
Chapter 2	The New Parson and His Parishioners (1579-1650)	10
Chapter 3	Bloxworth and the Civil War (1640-1675)	21
Chapter 4	Fluctuations of Fortune (1662-1699)	28
Chapter 5	The Trenchard Era (1689-1751)	33
Chapter 6	Jocelyn Pickard and Farming (1751-1800)	46
Chapter 7	Social Scenes - Agriculture in Decline (1800-1850)	61
Chapter 8	Progress and Problems (1850-1900)	71
Chapter 9	The Years of Change (1900-1945)	84
References and Notes		104

LIST OF MAPS AND ILLUSTRATIONS

The Chancel Door	4
The Hour Glass	5
Bloxworth Church	6
Three Farms in Tudor Times	7
Bloxworth House	11
Property surrounding the Glebe Land	13
The Chalice	14
Church Bells	14
Extract from the 1635 Churchwardens Presentments	15
The Inventory Of John Gosling 1624	18
Corfe Castle	22
The Charborough Icehouse	24
A Savage Shield	30
Sir John Trenchard	35
The Trenchard Memorial	36
Bound Oak	38
The Price of Material and Tailoring in 1688	42
From the Account Book of the Goold Family of Woodbury Hill	44
Bounding 1750	45
The Poor Law	47
The Prices of Miscellaneous Goods	52
Farming 1770-1771	55
Bloxworth Charity	57
Bloxworth Farming Return 1796	60
A Farm Cottage	65
The Parish of Bloxworth in 1845	67
Early Harvesting	72
The Madding Crowd	73
Octavius Pickard Cambridge	76
An Advertisement for Cider	77
Christmas Music	79
The Wedding of Miss Pickard-Cambridge	83
Horse and Trap Outside the Shop	85
A Village Scene	86
Bloxworth School - 1916	88
Bloxworth House	89
Ada Isabel Swyer	90
A Bloxworth Family	91
Bloxworth Land Girls	92
Bloxworth People	92
Glebe Cottages	93
The Meet at Bloxworth	94
A Tenancy Agreement	97
The Bloxworth Football Team	94
Bloxworth Cricket Team - 1933	100
Cricket - Bloxworth v Bere Regis	101
Bloxworth Home Guard - 1943	102
Forestry Work	103

PREFACE

This story was written to record something of the history of a village where my wife and I settled more than twenty years ago after a life of moving hither and thither. In the years when it was gradually taking shape, a very large number of people contributed to its contents. It all began in the early days when I attended a series of lectures by RNR Peers, the former Curator of the Dorset Museum. It developed significantly with visits to the Dorset Record Office when Miss Margaret Holmes was not only the senior Archivist but also a source of inspiration and advice. Lectures by JH Bettey, Jude James, R Machin and GJ Davies contributed towards a better understanding of Dorset's history.

Books and records from a wide variety of sources have also helped and many of the latter were found in the Wiltshire Record Office in Trowbridge and in the Public Record Office in Chancery Lane in London. In both cases, the staff could not have been more helpful and kind. Here, in the village, there has been no shortage of ideas. Mrs Fanny Gale and the late Mrs Nellie Gale provided local information covering much of the present century. Mr Ron Fancy, who went to school in the village, was always a fund of information as was Mrs Venetia Chattey whose family connections with the village go back to the time when the Trenchards owned the estate. Mrs Pearl Hewitt was kind enough to talk about her family who were stalwart Methodists amongst the farming community of Bloxworth. There were others too, and I apologise for not mentioning all their names.

I am particularly grateful to John Mennell who took most of the photographs and to my sister, Jean Benoy, who drew my attention to a number of sources in the Dorset Museum which I had overlooked.

Collecting and processing the many sources of information was fun. The hard work was recording it on paper and this task was undertaken with patience and understanding by my long-suffering wife, without whom there would have been no story and no account of the village's history.

INTRODUCTION

The problem about the writing of village history is 'where to begin'. People have been living close to Bloxworth in East Dorset since the Iron Age[1] but there is little evidence of who they were and for how long they survived. The Romans were in the area during their occupation of Britain but it is impossible to be sure whether they stayed in or near the village.[2] It is not until the days of the great Abbey of Cerne and that extraordinary land assessment, the Domesday Book, that there is evidence that a few people lived here where the farm land was valued at 'seven pounds and ten shillings'.

> *In King Edward's time it was taxed for five hides and a half. There is land to six ploughs. Of this there are two hides in the demesne and therein two ploughs, and three servi, and thirteen villeins and nine bordars, and seven cottagers with four ploughs and a half there are eight acres of meadow, and eight acres of wood, and pasture eight quarentens long and the same broad. It is worth seven pounds and ten shillings.*[3]

The farm land formed part of the estate of the Abbey at the Dissolution of the Monastery in 1539 when its value had risen to an estimated £26-15-6.

It was likely that Richard Savage and George Strangways had leased the estate from the Abbey before the Dissolution and they were probably fortunate that the land was not sought after by the many more important people who had influence amongst those who arranged the sale of the Abbey's lands. Nevertheless, they paid a good sum for the estate (£640-17-0) but it included a fishery at Hungerhill and some property which had belonged to Tewkesbury Abbey at Tarrant Monkton. There was also a smallholding which had formed part of the Cranborne Priory estate. The Savage family seems to have bought out the Strangways who continued to live to the north of the parish in the small hamlet of Winterborne Muston.[4]

This is the story of the village of Bloxworth after the Dissolution of the Monasteries in 1539. The story has been called 'Yonder Ground' - the name of a field in the parish - and it starts when the Savage family were taking over the estate and were to become a significant influence in the village.

CHAPTER 1
THE SIXTEENTH CENTURY - IN TUDOR TIMES (1539-1603)

It was in the Sixteenth Century when Henry VIII (1509-1547) was on the throne and relatively few people could read or write, that the story of Bloxworth begins to become clear. Earlier records showed that collections of the farms and small-holdings which comprised the village had been part of the property of the Monastery of Cerne Abbas. The Strode family had once been the principal tenants but they were succeeded by a family named Savage who had become the tenants at the time that Henry Vlll decided to improve his position by closing the monasteries in 1539 and selling their lands and property. It was the Savage family who became the main influence in the village for the next one hundred and fifty years.

At first, Richard Savage and his partner George Strangways were only the tenants but eventually ownership passed to William Savage, Richard's eldest son. There is little evidence and no map to show the layout of the farms and small-holdings but there were a large number of tenant farmers and signs of the existence of strip-fields can still be made out to the east of the old parsonage. These fields may have been the last examples of strip farming in the parish for there is little doubt that the enclosed field system was adopted in Bloxworth early in its history and was probably completed during the time that the estate was owned by the Savage family.

The size of the little farms and small-holdings varied and the rents depended both on the extent and quality of the land and the length of the tenancy. There were a number of small farms of about twenty-five acres in 1574 and part of the estate was farmed by five tenants whose property consisted of:

A moiety of the Manor of Bloxworth late called by the name of Strodes Landes in consideration of £313-6-8[1]

Thomas Clavell was the tenant of one of the smallest farms in this group, described as:

one tenement, lands, meadows and pastures in East Bloxworth for three lives at an annual rent of 40/-, 'two cople of capons' and other customary services

The most serious effect on the village was the upheaval in church affairs which followed when the King broke off relations with Rome. Henry VIII was not opposed to Roman Catholicism, only the failure of the Pope to agree with his

THE CHANCEL DOOR
The picture is of a dripstone - one of the two figures on each side of the little used door on the south side of the chancel in Bloxworth Church. It is probably the work of Richard Lockwood Boulton and formed part of the restoration work on the church in 1870. Richard Boulton was a well-known sculptor whose work can be found in many Dorset Churches. Photograph by Cynthia Sansom

marriage arrangements. Although an English translation of the Bible had been introduced there were few in Bloxworth who were sufficiently literate to read it.[2] In any case, there was little or no change to the well-known and understood Roman Catholic forms of service. During the short reign of Henry's son, the boy King Edward VI (1547-1553), a great number of changes were introduced - images and paintings were removed from churches, no more than two lights were allowed on the altar and the ringing of bells during Mass was forbidden. Instructions were given that a copy of the 'Book of Homilies' and the 'Paraphrases of Erasmas' were to be placed in each church.

Archbishop Cranmer had introduced an English Prayer Book in 1549 and three years later another English version of the Prayer Book was produced. Priests were allowed to marry and were not allowed to wear copes and vestments. Church plate was seized by the Government to raise money - policies which the village parsons would have found difficult to explain to their wondering flocks.[3] Then the young King died and was succeeded by his half-sister, the staunch Roman Catholic, Mary (1553-1558). Bishops were required to restore the old order, married priests lost their appointments, there was reconciliation with Rome and persecution of Protestants. It was no wonder that in the space of ten years between 1548 and 1558, Bloxworth had five different parsons.

In spite of these difficulties the church was and continued to be a most powerful influence in the village. It provided stability and continuity, it set standards of behaviour and morality and was in a sense the governing body of the community quite apart from being the centre of Christian faith. The church

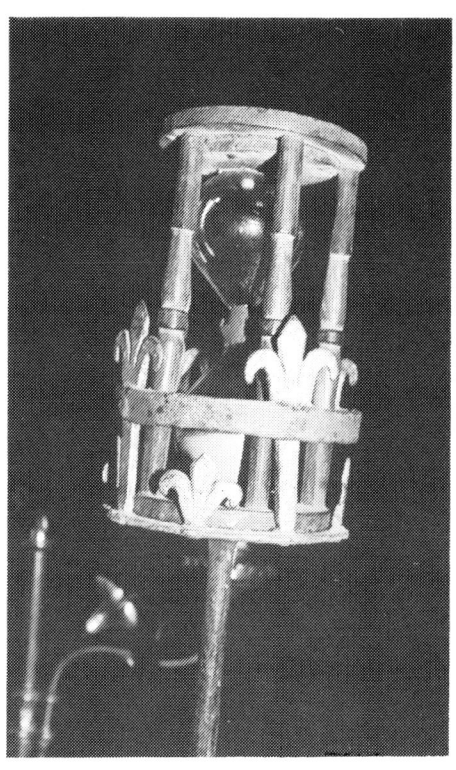

THE HOUR GLASS
The Hour Glass was placed in Bloxworth Church when the Savage family owned the estate and it stands on the Pulpit. It was a standard piece of furnishing in churches in former times to remind the parson during his sermons of the passage of time. Very few of the hour glasses have survived and the present one was damaged in an unlucky accident in the 1860s.

was supported by the owners and yeoman farmers and very few people absented themselves from the services. In 1599, Christian Curtis prepared her last will and testament and whilst the opening paragraph may have been normal practice, it is an example of religious conviction at the time;

> *In the name of God Amen the Eleventh Day of February in the year from the incarnation of our Lord Christ one thousand five hundred ninety and nine of Christian Curtis of Bloxworth in the County of Dorset widow being of good understanding and perfect memory (for which I praise my God) Do make my last Will and Testament in manner and form following. First I bequeath my soul into the hands of God my faithful Creator and loving Father Jesus Christ my Saviour and Redeemer the Holy Ghost my Comforter and Sanctifier and my body to the earth to be buried where it shall please the Lord to end my days assuredly believing and hoping that both my body and soul being redeemed by Jesus Christ shall for his merits and by the virtue of his resurrection be joined again together and obtain life everlasting.*[4]

Christian Curtis left a sum of three shillings and four pence for the maintenance and repair of the Parish Church.

BLOXWORTH CHURCH
The oldest part of the church is the doorway which lies beyond the porch which can be seen in this picture. The building dates from the Norman period although many believe that there was a church or chapel on the site from the earliest times. The sketch was drawn for the Parish Magazine by Jim Boyt of Winterborne Kingston.

A number of those who lived in Bloxworth left Wills and Testaments which have survived today. Even Henry Maker who failed to make a proper will before he died in 1573 was credited with the making of a 'nuncupative' will when shortly before his death and in the presence of witnesses he told them verbally how they should distribute his estate. Henry Maker was a tailor and he wanted his uncle to receive all his goods, chattles and any monies owing to him. The administrators of the will found that he was owed the not inconsiderable sum of £18-13-4 by two men, one from Turners Puddle and the other from Holton.

Edward Minion was the Bloxworth bee-keeper. At his death in 1589 he was worth the small sum of £8-10-2 but this included six acres of corn together with a cow and two horses. He made a written will seven days before he died specifying who should receive eight of his many bee-hives. His two married daughters were amongst the beneficiaries of his legacy and the remainder of his goods were to become the property of his widow, Margaret.

Some of the lists of property show the type of farming which was carried on in the village in Tudor times. The chalk downland to the north of the estate was

THREE FARMS IN TUDOR TIMES

Name	Jone Meder		Edward Prince		John Wheeler	
Date	June 20th 1575		Sep 26th 1587		May 4th 1596	
Occupation	Widow		Not Stated		Husbandman	
	Qty	Value	Qty	Value	Qty	Value
Stock						
Bullocks/Oxen			3	£6 -13 - 4	4	£10 - 0 - 0
Young Bullocks			3	2 - 0 - 0	6	3 - 10 - 0
Kine	2	£2 - 0 - 0	2	2 - 13 - 4	7	10 - 10 - 0
Heifers					3	4 - 0 - 0
Calves	2	11 - 8				
Horses/Colts	2	1 - 6 - 8	3/1	4 - 0 - 0	2	3 - 0 - 0
Sheep			19	2 - 0 - 0	60	12 - 0 - 0
Lambs					10	1 - 0 - 0
Pigs	2	16 - 0	3	15 - 0		
Crops						
Wheat (acres)	10	5 - 0 - 0	8	5 - 0 - 0	10	6 - 13 - 4
(bushels)					22	4 - 8 - 0
Barley (acres)	4	1 - 12 - 0	10	7 - 0 - 0	3	2 - 0 - 0*
(bushels)					44	5 - 10 - 0
Oats (acres)	2	12 - 0				
Rye (acres)	1	10 - 0				
Hay			#	2 - 0 - 0		
Dredge (acres)	2	12 - 0	2	1 - 0 - 0		
Fatches (acres)	½	10 - 0				
Peas (acres)	1					
Peas & Oats (acres)					3	1 - 0 - 0*
Total Value		13 - 10 - 4		35 - 1 - 8		63 - 11 - 4
Total including chattels		£17 - 18 -10		38 - 13 - 6		93 - 8 - 6

The details have been taken from the three inventories which were made when each of the individuals had died. The three farms which might be described as 'small, medium and large' but it is clear that the property of John Wheeler was given a higher value than that of Edward Prince.

Notes
* In the inventory the two items were combined. The breakdown here is an estimate.
# No quantity was stated.

particularly suitable for sheep but it was also possible to grow a variety of crops. Comparatively few cows were kept for there was no widespread distribution of milk although some of the surplus from local consumption was made into cheese. Oxen were widely used for ploughing and families usually kept a small number of pigs which after fattening would be killed and salted. Inevitably there were wide differences in the value of the goods owned by the small farmers or husbandmen at the time of their deaths. Jone Meder who died in 1574 was worth £17-18-10. Her near neighbour, John Wheeler, was a comparatively wealthy man who in 1596 left property to the value of £93-8-6.[5]

The organisation and administration of church affairs was unusual in that whilst the majority of Dorset Churches formed part of the Diocese of Bristol, a number of parishes including Bloxworth were made the responsibility of the Dean of Sarum and because of this arrangement were known, perhaps appropriately, as the Dean of Sarum's Peculiar. This had little effect on the general population but from time to time it certainly affected the Churchwardens who were appointed annually and chosen from amongst the better off members of the community. The Churchwardens (sometimes they were known as Guardians) were required to complete a written report or presentment to be delivered to the Dean's representative during his Annual Visitation to the parish. This usually took place during the summer months and a number of parishes were grouped together for convenience. Most of the Visitation Courts affecting Bloxworth took place in Bere Regis, a short ride or walk through Bere Wood, but on at least one occasion the Churchwardens were required to travel to Sherborne. The report provided the church authorities with a check on parish priests, particularly those who might not approve of the changes in the church's affairs which were caused by the disruption and later reconciliation with Rome. The presentment was also intended to give a general description of the state of repair of church buildings and the moral behaviour of the inhabitants of the parish. The majority of the reports at this time referred to the small number of people who in the worst cases had committed 'adulterye' but more often were described as 'living incontinently'. Some of them appear on more than one presentment but usually with the same partner. Occasionally there is a mention of the church fabric - an early report mentioned that the chancel was in need of repair at an estimated cost of twenty shillings in the 'default of Mr Austen Grene parson there' - he is mentioned again in connection with work required on the barns and buildings about the parsonage at an estimated cost of thirteen shillings and four pence. Once, in Tudor times, Anthony Wheeler and William Dyett, the Churchwardens, referred to an old village custom:[6]

> *Item we owght to have a Drinkyinge upon evry Easter day which hathe byun a custome tyme out of mynde our said parson refuseth to do the same*

Like many other men in his position, the Rector was able to afford a Curate and he probably left much of his work to his assistant. In 1576, Peter Benfield, the Curate appears in a report having been accused by one of the parishioners of unseemly behaviour with the complainant's wife. Whatever the merits of the case, the result was that the Reverend Austen Green was replaced in 1579 and nothing more was heard about the affair. Eighteen years later the appointment of Rector was filled by a man who was to remain in Bloxworth for fifty-five years. His name was Robert Welstead.

CHAPTER 2
THE NEW PARSON AND HIS PARISHIONERS (1579-1650)

Robert Welstead was about twenty-five years of age when he came to Bloxworth as a young newly-ordained clergyman. He had the advantage of a Dorset background for he came from Wimborne and, after a few years in the village, he married Anne Sawnders, a widow, in Bloxworth Church on November 28th 1603. Their daughter, also named Anne, was baptised in her father's Church in 1608. She was about sixteen and a half years old in 1624 when she married Benjamin Pitt, 'gent', and they had five children but her mother died in Bloxworth in 1640 before the last of her grandchildren was born. The Reverend Robert Welstead held no appointments outside Bloxworth and there is little doubt that he was familiar with all the villagers and equally well-known by all his parishioners. His theology and outlook tended towards the new thinking of the Puritans in what came to be called 'low church'. In the early days of his ministry in the village his activities often received adverse criticism particularly in the Churchwardens' formal presentments to the Dean.[1]

It seems that the parson not only failed to baptise children with the sign of the cross but also failed to read certain passages in church and, moreover, 'seldome wears the surplace'. In 1619, it was said that he neglected his duty in the reading of prayers on weekdays. In the following year the Churchwardens complained that the parson prevented them from having access to the parish registers and the same complaint was made in 1622. There was mention too that a Book of Homilies and Bishop Jewel's Apologia were not available in the church and that the Table of Degrees of Marriage which earlier had been reported as not available was later said to be 'Defaced and worme eaten soe that it is not to be reade & we intend shortly to have a newe one'. Repairs were needed to the tiling and timbers on the north side of the church to the value of twenty shillings 'in the fault of Mr Welsteede'.

There were, of course, village rows and Robert Welstead would have found himself in the role of arbiter, a thankless task for inevitably someone would be left uncomforted by the outcome. In 1614, a visitor from Charminster abused George Cole, the Parish Clerk, calling him a 'knave and other names in the church'. A few years later it seems that George Cole's successor did not qualify by age for the appointment:

We present that our newe parish Clerk is not 20 yeers of age according to the article, but in other things is proficient enough and such a one as we accept of

BLOXWORTH HOUSE
The house was built in Jacobean times in 1608 but the style is Elizabethan. The stables were built in the same century and alterations and additions were made later. The picture is of the south side of the house and is from a set of original lithographs (an early photographic printing process) by Pouncy called Dorsetshire Illustrated which was published in 1857

It was probably a challenge to the Rector for the report follows a paragraph in which the Churchwardens stated that it was the custom of the parish to choose 'our Churchwardens, Sidemen and Clerk ourselves'. Immorality continued to be a problem and the parson's task became more tiresome than usual when his son-in-law's servant was found to be the father of a child born out of wedlock. There were a number of similar cases. One concerned a couple living 'incontonently' and the circumstances were sufficiently unusual for the report to mention that the girl was only eleven years old. On another occasion the Churchwardens, having reported the birth of a child to an unmarried mother, subsequently blamed the family who had given the mother shelter, allowing her to leave the village without any 'Encyclical punishment first inflicted uppon her'.

There were cases involving those who had been excommunicated besides a number of less important matters. Some were named for receiving Holy

Communion whilst sitting down rather than kneeling. There were three occasions when men were reported for working on a Sunday and the Woolfries family from Marsh Farm were frequently mentioned for their failure to attend divine services. It would be easy to find fault with the parson, to blame him for many of the incidents and for his handling of them. It is as well to remember the difficult times in which he served the parish and the probably conservative attitudes of those who prepared the reports. In any case, village life often thrived on differences of opinion and quite small issues aroused great passion and concern. Robert Welstead must have dealt with these matters with a surer touch than many of the reports suggest.

In 1613, two members of the Savage family were Churchwardens and some form of instruction was received requiring them to prepare a description of the church's lands (glebe lands) in the village. Their acknowledgement to the Dean confirmed that they intended to undertake the work:

> *wee present that wee have not exhibited any terrier of the Gleibe lands of our parish but we desire a day to exhibit the same*

The Dean's Visitation took place on August 31st 1613 and by October 28th the Churchwardens had compiled so detailed a report that it is possible to compare their description with a map drawn some two hundred years later. Not only did the terrier describe the ground 'known to belong to the parsonage of Bloxworth' but it involved the tenant farmers on the periphery who added their knowledge and advice whilst the document was being prepared.

The Glebe Farm provided the parson with a source of food and an addition to his salary. Although some parsons had private incomes, many did not and depended for their livelihood on the produce from the glebe farm and the tithes from farmers in the parish. The terrier includes the phrase:

> *ther belonge to the sayd parsonage all manner of tythes within the sayd parish of Bloxworth*

Apart from the house and garden, the parsonage included a covert and orchard but it was also a farm and included a stable, 'backside' (farmyard) and barns in which the tithe crops would be stored. The parson was paid one tenth part of the produce either in cash or kind and although payment was resented it was probably no more resented than by those who had to pay taxes. It is clear that parsons needed to have a fair knowledge of farming practices but many had been brought up in the country and were familiar with country affairs. Apart from the fields to the south and south-east of the parsonage, the description of the Glebe includes a separate piece of land probably part of a field just to the north of what was to become known as East Bloxworth Farm (Manor Farm). It was a small plot of meadow known as the Parson's Acre, itself part of a larger field, Home Mead, and it seems that the field was included in the glebe specifically to provide the parsonage with hay:

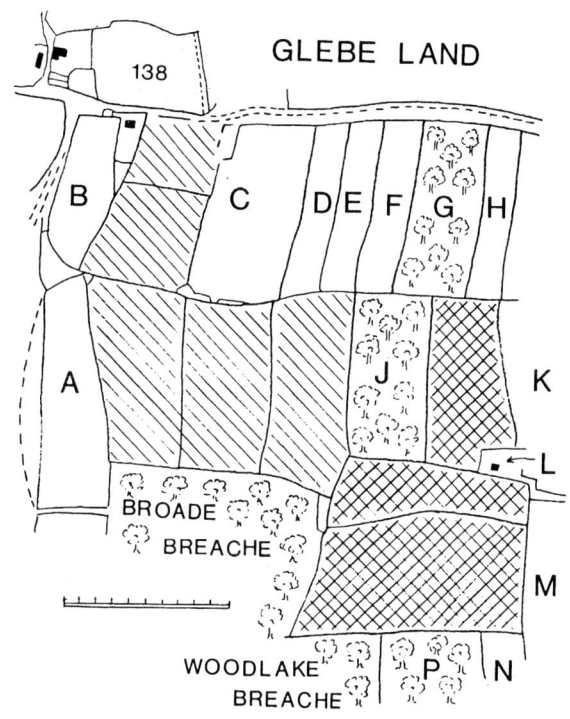

PROPERTY SURROUNDING THE GLEBE LAND - 1613

Field	Occupier	Type
A	Edward Vine	Lande
B	William Collins	Lande
C(*)	George Savage (Yeoman)	Lande
D(*)	William Cromplier	Close
E	William Stanlye	Close
F	William Collins	Part of a close
G	John Oliver	Litle copice
H	Edward Vine	Close
J	William Collins	Copice
K	Robert Holden	Lande
L	Christian Stroode (widow)	Cottage and garden
M	Woodlake Meade	Common Land
N	Edith Cosling (widow)	Close
P	Anthonye Durham	Litle copice

The property marked with an asterisk (*) was owned by Lady Wharton. The remaining land, including the woods named Broade Breache and Woodlake Breache, all belonged to George Savage (Yeoman).
The coppices (G,J and P) are almost exactly twice the size of the closes which may have originated as strip fields. Both shaded portions show the extent of the Glebe Farm in 1613. The glebe was changed in 1832 when the heavier shaded portions were exchanged for areas A,B,C,D and E together with Field No 138 and the adjacent farm buildings.

THE CHALICE
The Chalice is dated 1634 and is therefore a later addition to the "worst" one which the Church was allowed to keep by the Church Commissioners in 1551. It was lost for a time having been placed in the care and safe-keeping of a Bank. It was rediscovered when the Bank decided to initiate charges for the service. It is now kept in a private safe.

CHURCH BELLS
The pattern shown above is from one of the two existing bells in St Andrew's Church. The bell is extremely old - different authorities date it from either the 14th or 15th Centuries. The letters "MA" and "RI" probably represent "Mary" or "Maria" to whom the bell was dedicated. The lower case letters "all'a" is an abbreviation for the word "Alleluia". The second bell which is dated 1797 was presented to the Church by two of the Yeoman farmers.

There is a story that at one time there were three bells in the tower but one of them became cracked and was sold for sixteen shillings in 1780 with the intention that the money should be used for church repairs. It is rumoured that the money was misappropriated and used to provide a new brewing-copper for the manor house.

EXTRACT FROM THE 1635 CHURCHWARDENS' PRESENTMENTS

The presentments of ye Churchwardens of ye parish of Bloxworth

Concerninge ye Church	To ye first article we present that we have not Bishop Jewels apologie nor ye two books of homilies but they shalbe bought as soon as conveniently we may
	to the other branch of the table omnia bene
Concerninge ministers	To ye [Article] 19 that our minister for ye most pte doe declare unto ye parishioners what holy Dayes & Fasting Dayes are to be kept ye week followinge
Concerninge marage	To ye [Article] 2 that we have not in our church the table of Degrees concerning mariage
Concerninge Chyrurgions & midwives	To ye [Article] 2 that we have one Anne Hulet a poore wooman which doe sumtimes doe ye office of a mid wife but not sworne
Concerning parishioners	To ye [Article] 8 Thomas Frampton went to plough on St Marks Day last as it is reported
	To ye [Article] 24 that John Oliver ye younger as it is comonly famed hath comitted fornicon with one Joane Trew late of this parish but wheither they have given satisfaccon to your Court we knowe not
Concerning Scoolmasters	To ye [Articles 1 - 7] omnia bene

The owlde Churchwardens	The new Churchwardens
Robert Polden	John Oliver
Robert Melmoth	Matthew Cosins

* * * * *

There were a total of thirty-seven questions to which the churchwardens had to reply. To most of them the reply was 'omnia bene' and the answers have been omitted from the extract. In the interest of clarity, some of the spelling has been altered from the original version.

The question inquiring whether there were any Chyrurgions (Surgeons) or Schoolmasters is of interest. They were a category of people who might influence others.

> *... ther belonge unto the sayd parsonage the tithes of all the haye growing in so much of the sayd Home meade as is now in the occupation of the Customary tennants of the sayd George Savage of Bloxworth and all so growing in the twoe hammes of meadowe that are in the occupation of the hayward there, for the time being*[2]

There was one other privilege which had its origin in ancient custom which was for 'Common of pasture' in Bere Wood - also called the Forest of Bere - for the parson's herd of cattle. This large area of woodland to the west of the parish, outside the Bloxworth Parish boundary, was to become the basis of a legal dispute. In 1582, William Savage had complained that sixteen cows and two bulls had been 'unjustly detained' by John Rutter. The case eventually reached the Star Chamber in 1583 when it became described as a 'greate controversie' concerning the boundaries between the manors of Bloxworth which was owned by William Savage and Bere Regis which was the property of Thomas Turbervile. The evidence was that on November 7th 1582, one John Rutter, a servant of Turbervile and six others who were 'armed & arrayed with bills, pykes, staves' assaulted William Gover of Bloxworth grievously hurting him with a pyked staff and 'sett a mastive dogg' at him saying to the dog 'Holde'. There were claims, too, that on previous occasions servants of Turbervile 'armed and arrayed' had enclosed land belonging to Bloxworth, had moved boundary stones and had taken Bloxworth cattle and impounded them. Moreover, they had stopped up 'by wall & pale' both the highway from Bloxworth to Bere Regis called Cow Lane and also a footpath from 'Woodberrye Hill Downe to Bere, contrary to the liking of the inhabitants of Bloxworth & Queens tenants in Bere Regis'. There were further suggestions that some of Turbervile's men had committed perjury at earlier hearings on the boundary dispute. In all, twenty-four people contributed to the hearings some of which took place in Blandford. One outcome of the case was the agreement that William Savage had common of pasture rights in Bere Wood at all times of the year for 'commonable cattle/except sheep'. In 1615, a similar incident occured when Thomas Trew of Bere Regis 'took' eight young beasts owned by George Savage which had been turned out to graze in the wood.[3]

Bloxworth Farm was the main farm in the village although it was also referred to as Dyett's Farm, a reference to William Dyett, a former tenant.[4] A legal document drawn up in 1620, gives a full description of the property which had probably changed very little over a period of thirty years, possibly for much longer. It was a substantial farm and in 1620 was occupied by George Savage Gent - but he was not the owner of the land which consisted of:

Arable Land	97 acres
Pasture Land	21 acres in six fields
Meadow	14 acres
Unstated	12 acres (called "Smallers Breach")
Marsh	1 acre

It is not always easy to trace ownership and the additional complications of tenants and sub-tenants. By 1596, George Savage had become the tenant of the farm for a down payment of £400 at an Annual rent of £3-7-0, a copyhold agreement based on three lives - his own and that of his two sons, William and Richard. Four years after their father's death in 1610, Richard gave up his share of the farm to his elder brother for a payment of £30 per year for a period of seventy years.[5]

One of the parson's main duties was to attend to the dying and there is evidence that Robert Welstead was conscientious in this work. On three occasions he was present and helped those who had only a short time to live and had not made their last will and testament. Thirteen wills and some inventories have survived for Bloxworth people who died during the first half of the Seventeenth Century. They indicate to an extraordinary extent the minimum needs of individuals who, in most instances, had few possessions. Most of the wills were for the more prosperous members of the village - husbandmen or their widows. Even so, seven of them owned property which was less than £10 in value, four were assessed at between £10-£20 and only two were better off; Henry Lawrence was worth £37-14-9 when he died and Jone Throttle, a widow, was reported to have possessions worth just over £82.

The documents contain a variety of matters, some sad but many less so. Walter Collins in his nuncupative will on September 20th 1616 left a jerkin and a pair of breeches to his godson. Walter was buried nine days later. Just over ten months afterwards his widow, Avice, married again. Anne Derham received a kettle in the will of her grandmother but she only benefitted from a part share in the 'Biggest Blacke Howked Cow'. William Howlett died on the same day that he made his will owing £14 which had to be met in kind from his goods which were valued at £25. He had some connection with the fair at Woodbury Hill for amongst the list of his possessions was 'the stufe at wodberye hill' which was valued at £3.[6] On May 2nd 1602, Robert Welstead was involved in compiling the inventory for Henry Lawrence which included an unusual entry under the heading of debts:

Imprimis Thomas Meder oweth 18-0
It[em] he oweth 20 Bushells of malte eight bushells of wheate & eight bushells of barlye all which mony & corne is not dewe before the thirde of May anno domini 1602

Apart from the strange coincidence that Henry Lawrence died shortly before the debt was due to be repaid, the debtor was also a beneficiary in the will;

It[em] I give unto Thomas Meder my carte & sull and plowe stuffe & one acre of corne to be paid into him one moneth next of the death of my wife......

The final episode in this curious story was that Henry Lawrence's wife, Phyllis, survived him by only about ten days and their names follow each other in the Parish Burial Register.

THE INVENTORY OF JOHN COSLING 1624

The Ellmitory of the goods of John Cosling of Bloxworth who departed this life the eighteenth day of March Anno Domini 1624

		s	d
Imprimis his wearinge Parrell		1	6
It fower pillowes		3	0
It three blankets		3	0
It a bedsted			6
It old boords and a ladder			6
It tow tabell bordes		1	8
It a cubbard		5	0
It two chest and one coffer		10	0
It three trendels & one standord		1	0
It a brandit a gredion a tostinior			6
It a old spard two old hachets & other tolles		1	0
It a old kroke		1	0
It a chayer a chorch and two ceves			8
It a payle two covells		1	0
It two badd turnes		1	0
It a old cittell		1	0
It two pongers a caffer a salt		1	4
It a littell pigge		3	4
It old choyer			2

The who sume 37/6d

      WILLIAM SAVAGE JR
      JOHN LANNINGE (His mark)
      GEORGE SIMONTS (His mark)

(Note The total is incorrect and should read '37/2d')

Joane Loveridge was a widow and was one of very few whose possessions included a book - 'a Psalmes booke'. It is most unlikely that she was literate but no doubt the book was treasured and, in 1624, was an unusual piece of property for one whose goods and chattels were valued at only £7-10-1. The list of her possessions is an example of the very limited amount of wearing apparel owned by the average farm worker and his wife in the seventeenth century and the inventory includes only the following items of clothing:

	s-d
Two gowns	12-0
Two petticoats	5-0
Three waistcoats and one pair of bodices	4-0
Two cloaks	5-0
One hat	1-0

Thomas Loveridge remembered the poor people of the parish when he bequeathed four shillings to be distributed at the discretion of the overseers.[7] Edward Loveridge was another who failed to make a written will but his wishes were dictated to Robert Welstead and another witness and the parson was able to confirm in writing that 'when the said Edward Loveridge said this he was of good a[nd] pfit memery & under standing'. Occasionally an error occured when the will was copied. The widow, Grace Parlet, made a bequest to her sister, giving her 'all my linnen exyept one sheepe that hath now a marke which I appoynt for my shrowd' but Widow Parlet had no animals and the bequest must have referred to a marked sheet from her linen cupboard. She was also much concerned about the possibility of an early death caused by sickness but she lived for ten years after making her will. The wealthy Jone Trottle divided her property between her two married daughters but she disapproved of one of her sons-in-law and made special provisions to ensure that he could not benefit from his wife's inheritance. Edith Wheller's will is difficult to decipher for it is written phonetically in the Dorset dialect of the time. She distributed her goods and chattels to her family but is one of the few who did not overlook her servant:

> I Geve unto my mayde Margaret ..... awastecote one partelet anew Counerd Cercher anew apane

It was normal custom for men to make bequests which were to become effective after the death of their widows and John Wheller included a somewhat complicated instruction to this effect:

> I bequeth my coubord to my daughter Joan her [four] chilldren .... to be delivered wthin on mounth after the desseac of my wife or wthin on mounth after hir maryage if shee do marry and the couberd to be devided equally betwext them

Robert Welstead died in 1651 and is buried in a vault just outside the main entrance to Bloxworth Church. His influence over the parish and its affairs during the fifty-five years he was its Rector was significant although his lasting memory in modern times is the now faded inscription on his tomb:

> *Here lies that reverend orthodox divine,*
> *Grave Mr. Welsteed, Aged Seventy-Nine.*
> *He was the painful pastor of this place*
> *Fifty five yeeres compleate during which space*
> *None justly coulde his conversation wound*
> *Or's doctrine taint 'twas so sincere so sound*
> *Thus having his long threed of life well spunne*
> *'Twas cutt Novembers Tenth in fifty one.*

Whilst Robert Welstead concentrated on the cure of souls, the owner of the estate, George Savage, was devoting time to the siting and building of a manor house in keeping with his status as a country gentleman. The result was Bloxworth Manor, completed in 1608 and therefore described as Jacobean although it was designed on the 'E' pattern much favoured by those building country houses during the reign of Queen Elizabeth. The house is tucked into a valley on the north side of the village with Bere Wood protecting it from the west. It is a handsome house with stabling added during the Seventeenth Century and considerable alterations and additions at later dates. It must have caused enormous interest throughout the village and there is no doubt that it provided extra work and opportunities both during its construction and after it was completed.

CHAPTER 3
BLOXWORTH AND THE CIVIL WAR
(1640-1675)

There is no doubt that the inhabitants of Bloxworth were aware of the problems which faced King Charles I in his attempt to dominate Parliament. Fifty-two of them, male and over the age of eighteen, had declared the oath of protestation which, in 1641-42, required men to declare their opposition to Roman Catholicism and their support for the power and privileges of Parliament. In the oath there was a phrase referring to allegiance to the King but the country was divided between those who supported the Royalist cause and those who supported Parliament. In Dorset, the seaports of Poole, Weymouth, Portland and Lyme Regis and the principal towns, Dorchester, Sherborne, Blandford and Wareham were to become centres of military activity. Bloxworth people visiting the nearby Iron Age fort at Woolsbarrow could see the Royalist stronghold of Corfe Castle only ten and a half miles away.

The village itself had no military significance but amongst the population were two men, William Savage Esquire and Captain James Dewey who had close connections with those involved in politics. Moreover, Charborough Estate in the adjoining parish was the home of Sir Walter Erle, sometime Member of Parliament, who was to become one of the senior generals in the parliamentary cause and whose son was the Member of Parliament for Wareham in 1640-41. Those in the immediate area who might have favoured the Royalists were few and wisely kept their own counsel.

William Savage was the most influential man in Bloxworth. Like Sir Walter Erle and his son Thomas, he was a Justice of the Peace and was one of the original members of the Dorset Standing Committee which was founded by the Parliamentarians in 1644. The Committee was originally intended to co-ordinate the raising of money for the 'maintenance of the Army and to be likewise obedient to such further instructions as from time to time they shall receive from both Houses of Parliament'. Most of the money was raised by taking over the estates of those who were Roman Catholics (recusants) or pro-Royalist (delinquents). The estates were assessed in value and supporters of Parliament were allowed to become tenants and paid rent to the local Parliamentary Treasurer. Later it was found that many of those ejected from their estates had no funds to maintain either themselves or their families and many of them were allowed to receive one-third of the rent from their own properties. In the early days the Committee was given power to award payments for accounts and pensions, for example, to those who were wounded or to the relations of soldiers who had been killed. They also heard

CORFE CASTLE
There is no evidence that citizens of Bloxworth were involved in the battles around the Royalist-held Corfe Castle during the Civil War but the castle can be seen from high ground in the parish and at least two of the most prominent members of the village were closely associated with the Parliamentary cause. The castle must have been a fine sight until it was destroyed after its capture in 1645. The engraving is a view of the castle in 1643.

appeals by those whose estates had been sequestered and who considered that they had been unfairly treated. William Savage attended many committee meetings and in October 1646 he was awarded money for services rendered to parliament;[1]

> *Whereas it appeareth unto this Committee by sev'all notes produced that William Savage, Esq', hath advanced and sent in for the use and releefe of the souldiers within the garisons of Poole and Warham, in foode, fyreinge, woolle, hey and oates to the value of fortie nine pounds and nyne shillings and a penny; it is therefore ordered that the Treasurer of this Countie forthwith pay unto the said Mr. Savage the said sume of 49li 09s 0jd, for which this shall bee his warrant.*

William Savage became High Sheriff in 1648, no doubt in recognition for his services as a supporter of the Parliamentarians and not least for his work on the Dorset Standing Committee. A great deal of travelling was involved in the work for the Committee which met from time to time in different towns in the county. William Savage was one of the signatories to a letter from the Committee which was despatched from Shaston [Shaftesbury] on July 3rd 1646 in which complaints were made about the conduct of the Army in Dorset. It included the request 'therefore our humble suit to the Honourable House of Commons is, that there being noe enemie now visible in theise partes, wee may be freed of the intollerable burthen of the souldiers that now are amongst us...'. William Savage died in 1649 having been closely involved in the establishment of what became known as the Commonwealth when for a period of almost exactly eleven years (1649-1660), England became a Republic.

William Savage was a mature, steady and respected administrator. The other principle character from Bloxworth was James Dewey. At the start of the Civil War when he was only thirty-five, he became a widower when his wife, the former Mary Strangways of Muston, died suddenly leaving him with responsibility for their three young children. Little is known about him during the early stages of the war but he seems to have been an able and efficient soldier for he was later to receive prominence which must have been the result of early success. He held the rank of Captain and commanded a Troop of Cavalry available to be sent at short notice to wherever a show of force was needed. There was evidence of his service in April 1647 when the cases of two cavalry soldiers were considered by the Dorset Standing Committee. Neither of them had received any pay and both had subsequently become officers. They had been members of Colonel Brune's Regiment and during the early days had served in Captain Dewey's troop.[2]

In September 1646 he was awarded the sum of £32 'towards the satisfaccon of his disbursmts menconed in a debenter unto him given by this [Standing] Committee'. The money was to be found from the rent of 'Filloles Farme' sequestered from Jeffery Samways, described as a delinquent and thus a supporter of the Royalists. The farm lies just beyond the southern boundary of the parish of Bloxworth. In the following month, the Standing Committee directed that he should receive a further £30 from the Treasurer 'in pte of his disbursmts for the srvice of the State'. The sums of money were substantial for these times but larger amounts, like those paid to William Savage, were authorised for the provision of supplies. In 1647, the Committee authorised:

> *George Mullins of Bobbington [probably Bovington] in this Countie hath the publique fayth of the kingdome for feftie pounds and six shillings for horses, sheepe, wheat, cheeses, oats, and other provisions by him deliv'ed to Captaine Dewy and Mr. Thomas Hughes to the use of the State.....*

In March 1647, the Committee ordered the valuation of a farm at Keinson which had been sequestered from Mr Arundell who was described as a recusant or Roman Catholic. The following month Captain Dewey was authorised to rent the farm 'for one whole yeare' at a rent of £300 and subsequently William Arundell was allowed to receive one-third of the rent of his property. A year later the Committee found it necessary, no doubt as the result of an application by Mr Arundell, to order Captain Dewey to pay the rent which he owed.

There were other occasions when failure to carry out the decisions of the Committee were, not surprisingly, causing concern. A tenement in Corfe Mullen had been sequestered and allocated to Mr Morgan Blandford on condition that

> ## THE CHARBOROUGH ICEHOUSE
>
> The Icehouse - technically, it was an icewell - seems to have been the meeting place of those who planned to replace King James II with King William IV. The wording on the plaque above the building is reprinted below and it would be of interest to know the names of those who attended the meeting. One was probably Sir Thomas Trenchard whose brother and sister had both married into the Erle family. Sir Thomas Trenchard inherited Bloxworth in 1694 from his brother.
>
> Under this roof, in the year 1686,
> a set of patriotic gentlemen of the neighbourhood
> concerted the great plan of
> THE GLORIOUS REVOLUTION
> with the immortal King William;
> to whom we owe our deliverance
> from Popery and Slavery,
> and expulsion of the tyrant race of Stuarts;
> the restoration of our Liberty,
> the security of our Property,
> and establishment of National Honour.
> ENGLISHMEN,
> remember this glorious æra,
> and consider that your Liberties, procured
> by the virtues of your ancestors,
> must be maintained by yourselves !
> THOMAS ERLE DRAX
> erected this stone,
> in the year 1780.

he paid £40 per year to an officer who had lost his eyesight during the war; the money being intended as compensation. However, no money had been paid and the Committee ordered Mr Blandford to deliver up possession of the tenement and that if he failed to carry out the order 'then Captaine Dewy, or any other Commander in this Countie .... are heereby required to cause this order to bee observed'.

However well intentioned, it often took a very long time before accounts were settled. Such was the difficulty faced by Nicholas Symonds of Melbury Osmond whose problem was considered by the Committee in December 1648:

Whereas Capt. Dewy had and reciv' (about fower yeares since) .... fower cowes, price 12 pounds, for the use of the souldiers in the garrison of Warham, when it was a garrison for the pliamt, for which cowes the said

Symonds hath received noe pt of satisfaccon ....

and an order was made for him to be paid.

The accounting system was centralised, no doubt to try and reduce the opportunity for individuals to improve their personal finances. Parliamentary soldiers were not required to settle bills other than for their lodgings. There is little doubt that they often failed to meet their obligations and sometimes helped themselves to items to which they were not entitled:

> *In October 1648 upon the petition of John Hyne and other inhabitants of Portland the Treasurer is ordered to pay Hyne 33s - he having disbursed the same in candles for the use of the guards in the island; - and to defauke (substract) £8-11-0 from the pay of Captain Dewy's troop, being so much due from them to the said inhabitants for their quarter in Portland*

James Dewey was becoming increasingly noticed for his ability as a soldier and his dedication as a parliamentary supporter. In January 1650 he was a member of a small group who 'sat on a commission from the Council of State to give the Engagement at Blandford'. The matter concerned a number of men from Blandford who had been arrested for proclaiming that the Prince of Wales was King of England. The following month Dewey was appointed one of the three Sequestrian Commissioners for Dorset.[3] This group assumed responsibility for management of the property of Roman Catholics and Pro-Royalists and the effect was to replace the work carried out by the County Committee. The main reason for the change was that the Council of State in London was short of money, to some extent the result of delays in collecting rents and in the payment for services. The system was not wholly satisfactory and was changed again four years later when the group became subordinate to the Commissioner for Sequestration in London and, in order to encourage greater efficiency, county commissioners were allowed to retain as expenses twelve pence in every pound that was collected. James Dewey is said to have acquired the Minute Book of the Dorset Standing Committee which was eventually passed on to the Bankes family at Kingston Lacy.[4]

Many of the priests in the county were pro-Royalist, for the senior members of the Church were opposed to Puritan ideas and wished to re-establish some of the ceremonial and ritual of former days. Many considered that the strict and authoritarian Archbishop Laud was more Roman Catholic than Protestant. Bloxworth was fortunate that in 1642 the Reverend Robert Welstead had completed forty-five years as the Rector. His moderate attitude which had been severely criticised earlier in his ministry was now regarded with favour by the Parliamentarians. No doubt William Savage and James Dewey were an influence but there is no evidence that Robert Welstead was ever considered to be other than a supporter of the Parliamentary cause.

Others were less fortunate. During the latter part of the Civil War, when Dorset was free of the fighting, there was a constant urge from London to find new recusants and delinquents for not only were they enemies of the State but they were also a source of income. James Dewey carried out the searches diligently and it was a time when harshness was probably commonplace. Then as now, the reporting of incidents depended much on the point of view of the writer. Sometime in 1665, Dewey and James Baker decided to arrest Hancock Clark, son of the Rector of Todbere, near Sturminster Newton, who was staying in the Rectory with his father, Roger Clark. Accompanied by a Troop of Cavalry and a Company of Infantry they arrived at the Rectory at midnight to make the arrest:

> *But Hancock, upon notice of their arrival, leapt out of a back-window into the midst of the Horse in the orchard with his drawers, shirt, and one stocking on; and, being set upon, gave Dewey a dangerous blow with an iron pin of an axle; whilst the rest, in the darkness, were struck off their horses by the limb of an apple-tree. Hancock made good his escape ..... the enraged assailants are said to have taken Roger Clark the father, aged 70; to have bound him neck and heels until the blood ran out of his eyes; to have carried him forthwith to Sturminster-Newton Castle; and to have burned his fingers with matches - of which torture he was about six months in recovering*[5]

The Reverend Roger Clark occupied a living 'worth but £40 a year' and had not been sequestered but he seems to have been less frequently harassed than William Wake who was removed from his appointment as the Rector of Holy Trinity and Saint Michael's, Wareham, during the War. William Wake was an unusual character and a description of him written in 1635 suggests that he was a Royalist supporter and that he had little time for the rather staid, serious Parliamentarians:

> *Before I parted from this towne [Wareham] I had a free and generous entertainment from the honest, merry, and true-hearted parson there, both at his owne house, and in the towne, and enjoyed much mirth from him, and those honest gentlemen that then were come to visit him; he was both a good scholler and a good soldier, and an excellent drum-beating parson, his preparations, troops, and voluntaries, his marches, skirmishes, and retreats, he beats ad voluntatem* [6]

William Wake's military involvement was confirmed when he was discovered amongst the defenders of Sherborne Castle which was captured in August 1645. Not surprisingly he 'suffered much during the war' and his son, Captain William Wake, recorded circumstances in which James Dewey was involved;

> *And after the King's army were all suppressed, and garrisons taken and surrendered, my father came to live in Blandford, and with Mr Hooke, a sequestered divine, and others, kept up the discipline of the Church of England at Brinston Chapel, and, when prevented there, constantly in his own house, out of which [several names follow including that of James Dewey] and others, pulled him out of his bed, and kept him, a very infirm man, on their guards, and daily moved him with them as they were*

commanded from place to place; they afterwards brought a troop of dragoons to seize him, and such as frequented the prayers of the church....[7]

William Wake died in 1661 and he must have suffered for his loyalty and particular brand of militant Christianity. James Dewey prospered for a time. He was a Member of Parliament for Dorset in 1656-57 and for Wareham in 1659-1660. It is thought that he married for a second time but to whom and when is not clear. His activities during the Civil War would not have endeared him to many people, although it is surprising how many Parliamentarians prospered after the Restoration. He is mentioned in a legal wrangle over the payment of money for a marriage settlement between Mary Savage, the daughter of the 'Parson of Bloxworth' and Dewey's younger son. Sadness was to follow the legal proceedings for his daughter-in-law died in childbirth on Christmas Eve 1673 and James died not long after in 1675. His first wife, his daughter-in-law and James, himself, are all buried under the aisle in Bloxworth Church.

CHAPTER 4
FLUCTUATIONS OF FORTUNE (1662-1699)

The Restoration of the Monarchy in 1660 probably had little direct effect upon the village despite the close allegiance to Parliament during the Civil War but changes were to follow which would affect everyone in the community. The new measures started in 1662 when the government's need for more money led to the introduction of the Hearth Tax. The tax affected only the better off members of the village for no charge was to be paid by those living in cottages. A list of those who paid two shillings each year when the tax was first introduced included the names of those living in the Tithings of Bloxworth and Muston. Thirty-one people were involved, the majority having four or fewer fire-places but there were three houses with seven or eight and Mr Richard Savage was assessed to pay for fourteen hearths. A similar tax had been paid in ancient times - it had once been known as 'fumage' - a tax on smoke (chimneys) - but it was extremely unpopular chiefly because the collectors were entitled to visit and inspect the homes of those who were due to pay - a 17th Century version of the invasion of privacy. The system of taxing hearths was withdrawn in 1689.[1]

Wills continue to supply information about the background circumstances of the more affluent citizens. Edmund Galton, who had to pay the tax on three hearths, died quite suddenly and:

> *... did make and declare his last will & testamt Nuncupative in these Words following all the like in effecte ... Wch Words were soe declared in the psence of Credible witnes*

The names of the credible witnesses are not recorded but Edmund Galton, Husbandman, had considerable property. This included £46 worth of corn and a total of £96-15-6 for the benefit of his children. Elsewhere, there is a reminder that in every village the blacksmith was usually one of the most influential people. William Chubb was not a rich man but he made a written will more than twelve years before his death when he left half-a-crown to each of his two sons - not a large proportion of his assets which amounted to £47-15-8. Not surprisingly some of his property, kept in a shed, included his anvil, bellows and other equipment to the value of £15-15-8.

Thomas Vine, Yeoman, was another whose name appeared on the list of those due to pay Hearth Tax. He had two hearths, a modest number compared with his assets of £151-13-6. He died in January 1670-71 and seems to have handed over all his farm equipment, animals and other stock before his death. He was careful with his money; the two men who prepared his inventory found £109 in the house and discovered that he was owed a further sum of £22-18-0. Elizabeth Wheller was a spinster who was living with a relative when she died in 1672 and her property consisted only of her clothes, a feather bed and a sum of money but she had a pleasant idea when she appointed her brother Thomas to be her executor and instructed him:

> ... to bestow one dozen & one paire of white Glovs wth black ribbonds in them amongst my freinds as a memoriall of me & to bury me in my windeinge Sheete ...

The Churchwardens' reports to the Dean continued to be made at regular intervals although in May 1673 the wardens must have found it inconvenient to travel as far as Sherborne to present their very short statement. Nathaniel Fry was frequently reported for failing to mend a fence adjacent to the churchyard and for not attending the Communion Service at Easter but there are indications that the Churchwardens were reluctant to report anyone in the village for misbehaviour. In 1671, they wrote:

> ... wee the aforesaid Church wardings have nothing to present at present excepting som that have not Received the sacrament whose names wee cannot nominate without further examination...

There were occasional reports of children born out of wedlock and one complicated story which seems to have ended happily when the girl, having run away, returned just in time to be married the day before she gave birth to her son.

In 1679, one of the Churchwardens was George Savage and the well-worded and clearly written report shows that consideration had been given to the internal layout of the church and the convenience of those attending the services:

> *We present the Pulpitt and Readinge Deske of the pish Church of Bloxworth aforesaid to bee very inconveniently placed for many of the pishoners to hear the Minister it being now placed under The Arch between the Church and the Chancell and that the fittest place for the said pulpitt to bee placed in is between the two uppermost windowes on the South side of the Church in the seats where Robert Alner the younger (with others) doth usually sitt which will bee no prejudice to the said Robert Alner or to any other pson there being sufficient roome in the Church ...*

The moving of the pulpit and reading desk was probably connected with a major reconstruction of the church at about this time. For many years the condition of the north wall of the church was known to have been unsatisfactory and Sir George Savage had decided to rebuild it, at the same time adding a chapel with seating for his family and their friends. The family chapel included space underneath the flooring in which their coffins would rest inside the church. This excellent addition to the church was decorated with six coats of arms, painted with care directly on to the plaster of the interior walls. The paintings were based on an assumption that the Savages were related to a well-known family named

A SAVAGE SHIELD
There are seven painted shields on the walls of the family chapel in Bloxworth Church. One of them is hidden under the later addition of the memorial to Sir John Trenchard and the remainder are faded and difficult to decipher. Fortunately, drawings were made of the six shields and an article was written by James Salter in Volume X of the Dorset NH & AF Club Proceedings in 1889. In the article, the Savage family's entitlement to the heraldry is disproved but it also makes it clear that the paintings are both remarkable and unusual. The example shown above is that of 'Savage quartering Bower' (Sir George Savage was married to Ann Bower).

Rock-Savage but the designs contain errors which invalidate them in heraldic terms and discount any claim that they had any connection with the Rock-Savages. There is little doubt that Sir George Savage hoped to be remembered as the head of a well-connected family.[2]

There were other improvements in the church although argument about the dating has cast some doubt whether they were carried out during the 17th Century. The limestone font has a fleur-de-lys design upon it and this is repeated on the somewhat crudely made Hour Glass stand on the pulpit but the former has been described as 13th Century and the latter dated as 18th Century. Some believe that both items were placed in the church in Jacobean times and that they were part of the improvements made by Sir George Savage.[3]

* * * * *

In 1682, the Churchwardens were faced with an unusual problem involving the Savage family which they tried to resolve by presenting a special report to the Dean. They must have been told that the procedure was incorrect and that the matter should be raised at the next annual visitation. In May 1683, they referred once again to the incident which had taken place almost exactly seven months earlier on September 10th:

> *Imprimis Wee present George Savage gent for making a disturbance in the Church in time of divine Service & replyinge to the Minister you make a disturbance in the Church*

The delay in dealing with the matter by the Dean might have been associated with the theory that the passing of time would resolve the problem. It seems that the young George Savage, probably in his early twenties, had been indiscreet in more ways than one. Rumour has it that he seduced one of the family maidservants and, despite the protestations of his family, decided to marry her. An entry in the Marriage Register - 'One copell not plain to be seen' - was probably an attempt to disguise the liaison. Sadly it was not the only problem which was facing the Savage family. Sir George, in spite of his knighthood and skill as a lawyer had incurred debts amounting to £5772. This enormous figure consisted of twenty-one different sums of money varying from £100 to the highest figure of £800. Seventeen of the items were the result of court judgements for 'Debt or thereabouts besides Costs of suit'. Sir George could not raise the money and he was arrested. He avoided a prison cell, presumably because of his position and title, but he was kept in some form of arrest in the house of Henry Glover Esquire 'Marshall of the Court of Kings Bench and prison thereunto belonging'. Sir George was allowed to keep a servant and was charged £8 a month for meat, drink and lodging. It would be of interest to know how he allowed himself to become the victim of such a disagreeable situation and it is not entirely to his credit that he blamed members of his family for his predicament. In his will dated 1683 he writes:

> *... hoping for pardon for my sinns only as I forgive my greatest enemies and offenders even those my unnaturall though nearest Relations who by quarrells and controversies of their owne raiseing without any just cause for the same by mee given and by their conspireing to imprison my person have shortened my life and subverted my family*

This does not explain how the debts occured but shows that no members of his family were prepared to finance his losses. Sir George found this incomprehensible and he included in the will a further attack upon his wife and her relations:

> *... but for the preventing those mischeifes to others which have unhappiely orfallen myselfe I leave this advice to my sonnes Viz that if every they marry and attaine to a settlememt or transefers in the world as they hope to live comfortably with their wives and to be happy in dutifull children they make choise of women of agreeable principles and inclination with their own and admitt neither mother, mother in law nor any other their neare relations to reside or Cohabit with them in their families that soe noe diversitie of opinions or humours or disputes of domestick or other*

consernes may set them at variance one with another or lessen in them that respect and affection which should mutally bee betweene such alliances...

The will continues in less bitter terms dealing with the education and upbringing of his sons and payment to be made to Mr and Mrs Glover and their servants including an acknowledgement to Henry Glover of 'his greate respect and kindnesse towards mee'. There was also extensive advice on the reorganisation of Bloxworth's three farms - Dyetts, Middle Farm and Zouches - and mention of the recent sale of the Parsonage at Tarrant Monkton[4] to Henry Trenchard Esquire - presumably to try and raise some of the money which he owed. Perhaps the saddest part of the story was the directions given to his son George and to Henry Glover about his funeral:

...appointing my body to be interred in my Isle adjoyning to the parish Church of Bloxworth aforesaid but with as much privacy and as little expense as my decently bee And if I shall happen to die in the custody of the said Henry Glover my sonne George not being present or neere mee at the time of my decease to undertake such care as aforesaid it is my request to the said Henry Glover that hee will cause my body to bee Conveyed withall convenience spad and in a private (but decent) manner to my mothers house in Bloxworth aforesaid in order to the interrmt thereof accordingly as is herein before dirated and appointed

Sir George Savage died in 1683 and was buried in Bloxworth as he had requested. His debts became the responsibility of his family and it was clear that the estate, built up and developed over such a long time, would have to be sold. No doubt the village was disconcerted by these matters and some must have supported the Savages whilst others opposed them. In 1685, dissension spread to the Church when fifteen people did not receive Holy Communion at the Easter Service. Amongst the group was Nathaniel Fry whose opposition to the Church was well-known but the list also included the son of one of the Churchwardens and the wife and family of the Rector. In 1689, William and George Savage signed a legal document transferring the estate to Henry Trenchard for £9,200 confirming a sale which had been agreed during the previous year. The Reverend John Savage - known as 'The Elder' - continued to manage the affairs of the church in Bloxworth until his death in 1698 when he was succeeded by his son, also named John. The death of Sir George was the end of an era in the village, although the name of Savage continues to appear in church records until 1763. Now there was a new Lord of the Manor and a new influence in the affairs of the village. The presentments to the Dean of Sarum became less dramatic, dealing usually with the state of the churchyard and such is the entry in 1699 at the turn of the century:

Item We present severall Lotts in ye Church yard which ar in Decay and ought to be Repayerd

CHAPTER 5
THE TRENCHARD ERA (1689-1751)

The village of Bloxworth now became associated with one of Dorset's oldest and most prosperous families. The estate was sold to Henry Trenchard, a lawyer whose practice was in the Middle Temple in London. Members of the Trenchard family owned several houses. One was at Wolfeton, just north of Dorchester, another at Warmwell, six miles north-east of Weymouth and there was a third estate at Lytchett Matravers on the outskirts of Charborough Park. In the days when wealthy families arranged suitable marriages to maintain or extend their influence, the Trenchards were especially careful to enlarge their properties. Henry's sister Ann married Walter Erle of Charborough whilst his eldest brother Thomas was married to Anne Erle. Similar arrangements were to affect the management of Bloxworth for the next two hundred and fifty years.

Henry Trenchard must have been aware of Sir George Savage's financial problems and it is tempting to assume that he acquired the estate at a bargain price. Certainly the legal matters were completed carefully and at length and there is no suggestion that Henry obtained an unfair advantage. The Savages, Erles of Charborough and the Trenchards were known to each other. All had held important posts during the Civil War and had the same interests in preserving their positions during the uneasy times which followed the Restoration of the Monarchy.

Henry Trenchard was a bachelor and a fifth son so he was unlikely to succeed to the best of the Trenchard properties. Under normal circumstances he would have left his estate to the head of the family but his eldest brother, Thomas, had just died. Henry's fairly short will was completed just before his death and was written in 1694 only four days before he was buried at Bloxworth. Henry left a handsome legacy of £400 to John Southby, the son of his sister Mary, and he bequeathed his estate to his brother John who lived in the Trenchard property at Lytchett Matravers:

Imprimis I constitute and make my loving brother Sir John Trenchard my sole Executor and doe give and bequeath unto him all my lands tenemts and hereditaments whatsoever I doe possesse in the County aforesaid hee first paying my debts and Legatyes....

Sir John Trenchard has been described as 'a calm and sedate man, and much more moderate than could have been expected, since he had been a leading man in a party. He had too great a regard for the stars, and too little for religion'. However it is doubtful whether he was either moderate or particularly sedate. His father and uncle had been severely criticised for their activities in the Civil War and there is little doubt that Sir John had inherited much of their spirit for he had already been accused of involvement with the Duke of Monmouth in the latter's attempt to raise a rebellion in the West Country. He must have had anxious moments in 1685 when he had been dining with an old family friend in Somerset:

> *He was at dinner with Mr. William Speke at Ilminster, when advice came of the defeat of the Duke of Monmouth at Sedgemore. Mr. Trenchard [later Sir John] immediately mounted his horse, and advised Mr. Speke to do the same, lest he should be seized and hanged for his attachment to the duke. Mr. Trenchard reached Litchet; but instead of going to his house, concealed himself in the lodge of the park belonging to the keeper, whom he sent to secure him a passage on board a vessel at Weymouth. Tradition says, at the moment he was embarking, his friend Speke was hanging before his own door at Ilminster*[1]

Sir John did not acquire Bloxworth until many years after these events and he must have spent many years abroad or in hiding to avoid a similar fate to William Speke. He was devoted to the Protestant cause and is reported to have been closely concerned with arranging the details for King William and Queen Mary to succeed James II in 1689. Trenchard was knighted and became the Chief Justice of Chester, Secretary of State to the King and a Sergeant at Law to their Majesties. It is unlikely that he found much time for the detailed affairs of the village of Bloxworth but when he died in 1695, a handsome memorial was placed in what had hitherto been the Savage Family Chapel in Saint Andrew's Church. Sir John's personal estate was valued at £11,804-3-2 and the funeral arrangements which were made by his widow were appropriate to his high standing. Some of the costs were:

Wages for seven menservants and mourning for them	
Wages for six maidservants and mourning for them	
Mourning clothe for near relatives	£80-18-6
Mourning for deceased's chaplain	£10
Putting part of the house in mourning	£10
Captain Pitts for mourning rings	£36- 2-0
Mourning for Lady Phillipp and her seven children	£24- 0-0
Captain Thomas Pitt for diet and lodging when Mr George and Mrs Elizabeth Trenchard had small pox	£28-13-9

There were also medical charges and payments for two miscellaneous items:

Mr Charles Bate, the apothecary	£33- 0-0
Mr Chase, the apothecary	£3- 8-0
Mr George Trenchard's schooling at Kensington	10-0
'For coffee milk water & night capps'	16-0

SIR JOHN TRENCHARD
The inscription under the picture reads 'Sir John Trenchard Knt of Bloxworth in Dorsetshire principal Secretary of State to King William the Third. To John Trenchard Esqr this Plate Engraved from a Miniature Picture by Ozias Humphrys after the Original is gratefully inscribed by Cantlo Bastland.'

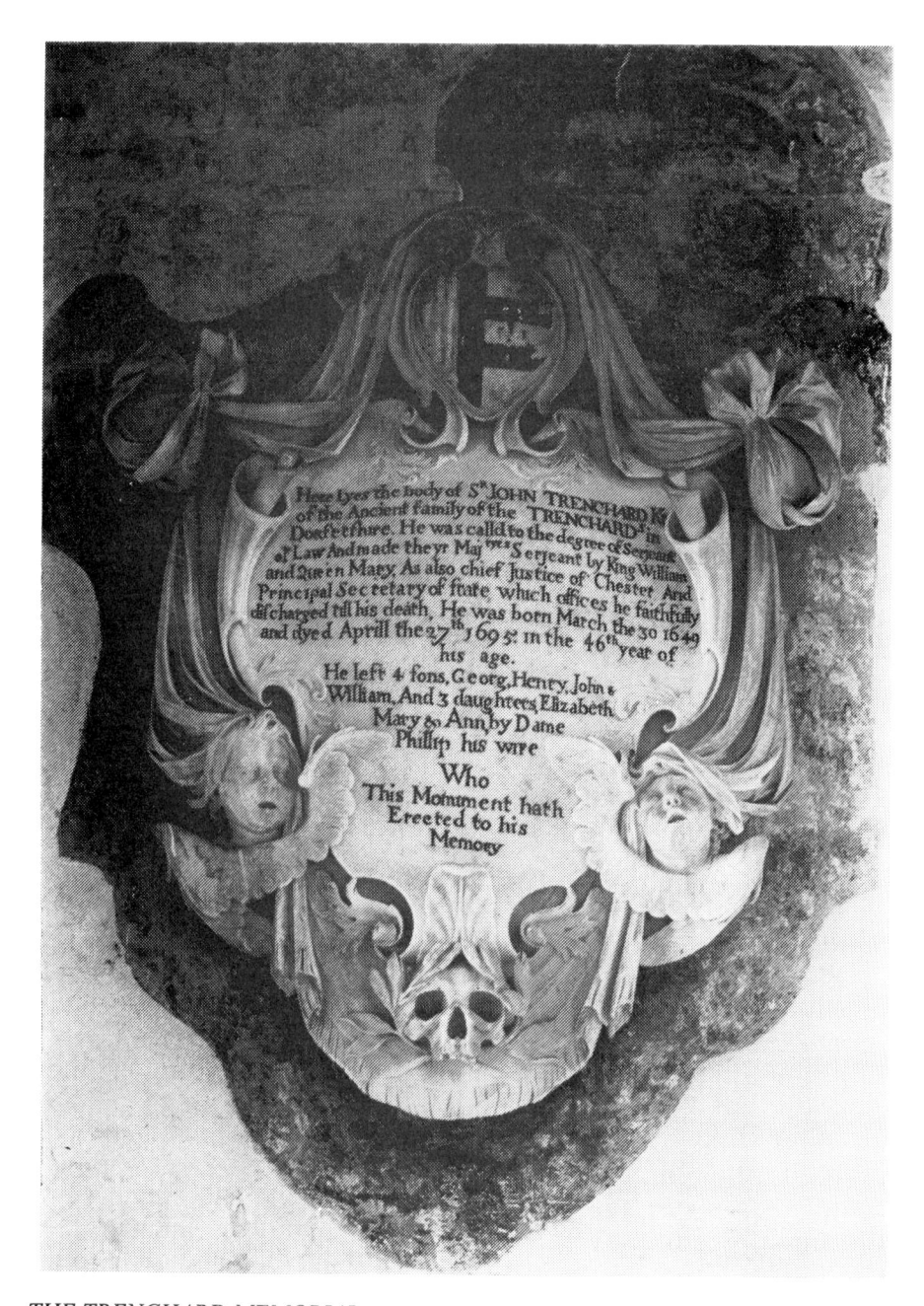

THE TRENCHARD MEMORIAL
The Memorial was erected on top of one of the Savage family shields in the north chapel in Bloxworth Church. About ten years after Sir John's death, Dame Phillip(a) married Daniel Sadler, a distant relation of the Trenchard family. Daniel Sadler died only a few years later and was buried in Bloxworth Churchyard in 1709.

Whether Bloxworth had formed part of Henry Trenchard's 'lands, tenemts and hereditaments' is in doubt. In 1705, Lady Phillipp Trenchard claimed that her late husband, Sir John, had bought the Bloxworth estate from Henry for £6500 and made other arrangements which were to the advantage of herself and others. The outcome did not affect the inheritance of Bloxworth by George Trenchard, Sir John and Dame Phillipp's eldest son. George Trenchard described himself as from Bloxworth and Lytchett Matravers but it is likely that he continued to live in the family home in nearby Lytchett. His mother, Dame Phillipp, may have moved into Bloxworth House but within a year she had married Daniel Sadler, a merchant and a distant relative of the Trenchard family[2]. Meanwhile the Trenchards of Wolfeton extended their influence when Colonel Thomas Trenchard married Elizabeth Henning, an heiress whose property was situated on the fringes of the attractive village of Poxwell, five miles north-east of Weymouth. Their only daughter Mary, was baptised in Lytchett Matravers Church in 1698. It was understandable that the two families should be drawn close together but the association was to become closer still. Colonel Thomas Trenchard died at the early age of thirty-two and in his will specified that his daughter, Mary, should marry one of the sons of his uncle, Sir John Trenchard. The marriage of George and Mary was a success if the size of their family was a measure of stability for they had eleven children. The eldest daughter, Henrietta, born in 1715, eventually married and became the second wife of Mr Jocelyn Pickard. It was they who became the new owners of the Bloxworth estate.[3]

The majority of those who lived in the village were more concerned in preserving the normal order of things than worrying about the change of ownership. From 1674 the rights and responsibilities of everyone in the village were recorded in the 'Court Booke of the Mannor of Bloxworth'. The Court met each year and solemnly confirmed those rights:

> *"... all Copyholders shall have timber for their use by assignment*
> *... all Pollards shall belong to the tenants*
> *... no cottages to have more than 3000 turves no any common of pasture*
> *... no cattle shall be turned into the lanes without a follower under the penalty of 20/- to be levied on each offender*
> *... neither Farm nor Parsonage have an pasture in the common*
> *... neither the Lord or Tennant shall sell or give any Turves or Furze out of the Common*
> *... no Piggs shall be turned into the streets without a ring or buckle under the penalty of 5/-*
> *... no Ducks or Goose shall be turned into the street or common under the penalty of 15/-*
> *... neither the owner occupier or tenant of Bloxworth Farm hath any Right to cut the underwood on Bloxworth Common"*

The Court was administered by the Homage - an ancient term describing the jury of three men whose task was to run the Court. Apart from recording the Rights

BOUND OAK
The drawing together with an article by Octavius Pickard Cambridge appeared in Volume III (1879) of the Proceedings of the DNH&AF Club. The oak tree stood by the right of way and marked the boundary between Bloxworth and Bere Regis. The tree remained in position until it was replaced in the 1970s.

which were repeated each year with little variation, the Homage also listened to 'Complaints' and 'Essoignes' [suggestions], if any.[4] Few of these were recorded but an occasional addition to the list suggests that more was discussed than the minutes indicate:

> *.. no person shall take up and carry out of the Common any cold dung under the penalty of twenty shillings to be levied against each offender*

The Homage or Court Baron were responsible members of the community and the meetings were attended by those whose interests were served by the proceedings. There were ten copyholders, twenty-five lease holders and one free holder at the meeting in November 1733 and this confirms that although there were only three main farms in Bloxworth at the time, there was also a comparatively large number of part time smallholders in the community.

The absence of the Lord of the Manor meant that the administration of the village continued to be the responsibility of the yeomen farmers, churchwardens and the parson. The restoration work had removed some of the problems in the church but in 1701 the porch and chancel door were 'out of repaire' and three years later reports continued about the churchyard and its fence:

> .. severall Lotts of fence about our Churchyard are yett out of repair occasioned by the fall of trees which grow in the fence & that the said Lotts have formerly been repaired by the Owners of the Demeasnes of the Mannor of Bloxworth

In 1714, the parson in Bloxworth was the Reverend John Savage and his Churchwardens, normally appointed for one year, were Benjamin Watts and Robert Manuel, both well-established Yeoman farmers. In those days the tithe was a significant and unwelcome tax and it seems that the Parson intended to introduce changes which might cause some resentment. The Churchwardens decided to provide the Parson with a detailed description of the existing tithes and an explanation of the system in existence for electing Churchwardens:[5]

> That it was ever the Custom of Bloxworth parish to Chuse Church Wardens without the Minister And this we Testifie to be the Antient Custome of the Parish of Bloxworth for 60 Years and upwards ...

The document started with the words 'We present the Minister of Bloxworth to keep a Bull and a Boar according to the Antient custom of this our Parish ...' and it continued with the amounts to be paid:

For tythe of a garden	2d
For Cow white for one Cow	1d
A person having but Seven Calves the Seventh is the Minister is to have the Seventh; only the Minister must give to the owner of the calf	1½d
if any kill a Calfe the Minister must have the left Shoulder; but if any Wean a Calfe, the Minister must have	½d
if any sell a Calfe the Minister must have	2d
if any having Seaven Lambs the Seventh is the Minister's only the Minister must pay the owner	1½d
For the fall of a Colt, the Minister is to have	1d
For the offerings for a Single man	2d

For the offerings for a Man and his Wife	1½d
All hedge Rows being not a Pole over is not Tythable	
That was never the Custom to Tythe Bees nor honey	
if any person have Seven Swine in a year, the Minister must have one of them; only the Minister must pay to the owner	1½d
if any person have but, 6 swine fallen the owner must pay to the Minister a halfe-peny for each	
If any Couples are Sold before Marks Day, the fall of every Lamb	½d

The Churchwardens may have had difficulty in finding others to put their names to this document for there are only four witnesses. These included a man from Bloxworth who had frequently been 'presented' for not attending church services at Easter. Another of the witnesses lived outside the parish but the absence of witnesses may have been to avoid recriminations rather than expressing disagreement with the proposal. Both Churchwardens signed their names to the following note at the end of the document:

All other Things is well to The Best of our Knowlege

Witness our Honest Church Wardens.

At the beginning of the 18th Century, there was a significant improvement in literacy amongst the leading members of the village a number of whom had property or tenancies outside the parish boundaries. This level of prosperity must have been the envy of many of their farm workers. William Alner who died in 1712 had possessions which were worth just over £180 including his farm equipment, corn and stock which amounted to £136-9-0. In his will of 1717, Henry Reeves mentions his house in Lytchett Minster. Joseph Jefferies wrote a complicated will in 1728 in which he disposed of leasehold estates in Tarrant Rushton and Sherford together with leasehold and copyhold estates in Bloxworth. Elizabeth Alner, who was a widow, specified that 'the rents and profitts of a certaine Copyhold Tenement at Puddle Hinton with the Lands thereunto belonging' should be used by her daughter, Elizabeth Strangeman, for the care of her brother 'who is now under a distraction of mind'. Elizabeth Strangeman died only six years after her mother leaving 'Part of the Goods belonging to me at Winterburn Kingston' to her son but it is not clear what became of her mentally disturbed brother. John Hucker was a carpenter with both a 'Leasehold Messuage' in Bloxworth and also 'Houses Buildings Lande & Heritaments' in Wareham. His son, George, was the principle benefactor and took over from his father as a carpenter in the village. Benjamin Watts, whose name appears on many old documents, had interests in Hyde, whilst another Yeoman and contemporary, David Abbott held a Leasehold Tenement in Winterborne Stickland.[6]

One of the great men of the village at this time was Robert Manuell. In 1734, when he was forty he had not made a will but on June 27th there were four people in his house when he was:

... suddenly seized for Death We whose Names are underwritten being then present heard him the Said Robert Manuell who was then of Sound Mind and Memory make this his Last Will and Testament in these following Expressions or Words to the Same Tendency or Purport ...

Robert Manuell then made three bequests and the witnesses added the following words:

All and Every of which Expressions or words to the Same tendency and purport He the Said Robert Manuell at least Three times repeated in our hearing ...

Robert Manuell had been married but there are no records giving any details about his wife. It is clear they had no children and he left the balance of his property to his brother Joseph.

The majority of people maintained a standard of living very little higher than subsistence level. Each cottager had a large garden in which they grew vegetables and many kept a pig and chickens. Circumstances meant that the elderly, whose working days were over, depended on their children for care and attention. Sometimes individuals could not manage and the parish became responsible for looking after them. Like most towns and villages, Bloxworth had a Poor House and in 1722 it was in need of renovation.[7]

Charges laid out on the Parish House

for 1000 bricks	10 - 0
for 5 bushells of lime	2 - 6
for 4 days work for myself	6 - 0
for 2 days work for Joseph Miller	2 - 4
for 2 boys per day work at 8d per day	3 - 4
for carriage of bricks and earth to Thomas Frampton	3 - 0

The work of looking after those who had nobody to care for them was the responsibility of two men appointed officially as 'Overseers of the Poor'. It was their responsibility to fix the rate of relief which varied from 14/2d paid by the Lord of the Manor to a charge of 3d paid by some of the tenants. In 1663, thirty people contributed a total of £3-10-0 and the money was collected three or four times a year depending on the number of people needing help and the extent of the aid which was provided. In 1720, some paid nine times whilst others were charged seven or eight times the basic rate. Two years later, when extra funds were needed, fourteen payments were made.

The money received from the rate was spent in a variety of ways. Part of it was for the destruction of vermin:

> ### THE PRICE OF MATERIAL AND TAILORING IN 1688
>
> | | s - d |
> |---|---|
> | 3 yards of cloth to make a suit | 10 - 0 |
> | 2 yards of serge | 50 - 6 |
> | 3 ells of canvas to make drawers | 2 - 0 |
> | 3 ells of canvas to make two shirts | 3 - 9 |
> | 1 ells of canvas for a frock | 1 - 6 |
> | For buttons, thread and tape | 7 |
> | For making a suit, two wascotes, two paire of drawers and a frock and buttens | 4 - 0 |
> | For making two shirts | 6 |
> | For a hat | 2 - 0 |
> | For two paire of shoes | 4 -10 |
> | For one paire of stockens | 1 - 2 |
> | For two neckcloths | 1 - 0 |
>
> The prices have been taken from the Bloxworth Poor Relief Book in 1688. They refer to the making of clothes for George Melmor (probably Melmouth), the youngest of four children who became orphans when their father died in January 1677-78 and their mother died in 1681. George would have been twelve in 1688 and needed good clothes when he began full time employment.

1700	Two Pole Cats heads	8d
	Two dozen Sparrows heads	4d
1706	Two foxes heads	2 - 0d[8]

John Hucker, the carpenter, was paid 3/- for mending a gate at Rushmore and on another occasion, 3/6 for repairing a bridge. He also received payment for making coffins. One reason for the increased rates was for the maintenance of two poor members of the Savage family, a widowed mother and her daughter, both known as Jane. In 1719, the mother was paid £2-5-0 for thirty weeks pay and subsequently she received 4/- each month until her death in October 1721. John Hucker was paid 10/- which covered both the cost of her coffin and also for ringing the church bell at her funeral. Her daughter, who was probably an adult and unable to look after herself, continued to receive aid from the parish. Much of the time she was cared for by John Daves who received 10/- per month for the work and two doctors Dr Gibbard and Dr Sims, were both consulted about her condition and received payment for their advice. She spent sometime in Halstock and although the reason for this is not clear, it is likely that it was connected with her medical treatment. Visits to the doctors and to Halstock also incurred charges for the journeys:

For my horse and expense going to Halstock	7 - 0
For keeping of Jane Savage at Halstock	18 - 0
Paid for John Hucker for his horse and himself to fetch Jane Savage	5 - 0
For my horse and expense in fetching Jane home	11 - 6

Jane died in 1724 and her coffin was made by George Hucker - probably John's fifteen year old son.

Another family fell on hard times in the 1720's and the entries in the book make sad reading. Poor Thomas Freeman was buried on January 3rd 1721 and the expences were paid for by the overseers of the poor:

"It[em] paid vales wife and bubberys wife for laying out Thos Freeman and washing his close	3 - 0
It[em] paid Elner Long for a shrood for Tho Freeman[9]	3 - 4
It[em] paid John Hocker for a coffin and diging a grave and ringing the bell for Tho Freeman	11 - 0

* * * * *

A mile and a half to the west of Bloxworth church, standing between Bere Wood and the town of Bere Regis is an Iron Age Fort and the site for many centuries of the Woodbury Hill Fair which took place over five days in September each year, each day being set aside for particular activities:

> September 18th Wholesale Day
> 19th Gentlefolks Day
> 20th All Folks Day
> 21st Sheep Fair Day
> 22nd Pack and Penny Day

It was the largest fair in the south of England and attracted visitors and traders from as far afield as the Midlands and Suffolk and its effect on the surrounding countryside was of great significance and importance. Its influence had begun to decline in the early part of the 17th Century and tolls which had formerly amounted to more than £100 had been reduced to £30 or £40 by 1730. Nevertheless, there continued to be much interest in what provided both a trading centre and a source of amusement and fun. On top of Woodbury Hill there was a collection of permanent wooden booths or cabins - they were known locally as 'bowers' - and from time to time some of the bowers were owned by Bloxworth people, amongst them Elizabeth Strangeman, who in her will in 1739 mentioned:

Item I Give my Son John The Bower at Woodbury Hill at the Age of Twenty One Years[10]

From the Account Book of the Goold Family of Woodbury Hill

*Mememberandum Conserning
June ye 6 = 1750 Beerfolks
& bloxworth people went a
bounding together into ye east
Coman
we begun at ye ditch betwen
new close & beerhambrech
ye first stone is by a homing
bush by ye way side :+: the
next stone is in ye medle of ye
pond :+: ye next is by a homg bush
about a 100 or a 100 & 20 goad
:+: ye next stone is by ye way sid
to ye left of ye way about a 100
or a 100 & 20 goad:+: ye next stons
are about a 100 or a 100 & 20
asunder theare are 2 stones
about 16 goad asunder one west
and ye other east to part hide
and beer ye east is to part
bloxworth and beer
bounding
then we goes down to the
hedes corner and from yt
thear is oak tree bouns a
little ways from hide barn
then from yt we goes to a oak tre
in glasburys hedge & from
thence we goe up ye hill &
thear 2 holes & when we
are a top of ye hill we goes
on to thomas hardys grave
and from thense we go on
to Bouenton stone by Dorchestr
way :+: & from yt to a little pond
upon ye left hand of ye way coming from
bouenton stone :+: and behether yt is a
nother pond in ye medle is a boun
stone & from yt about a 80 or a
100 goad is another bound stone*

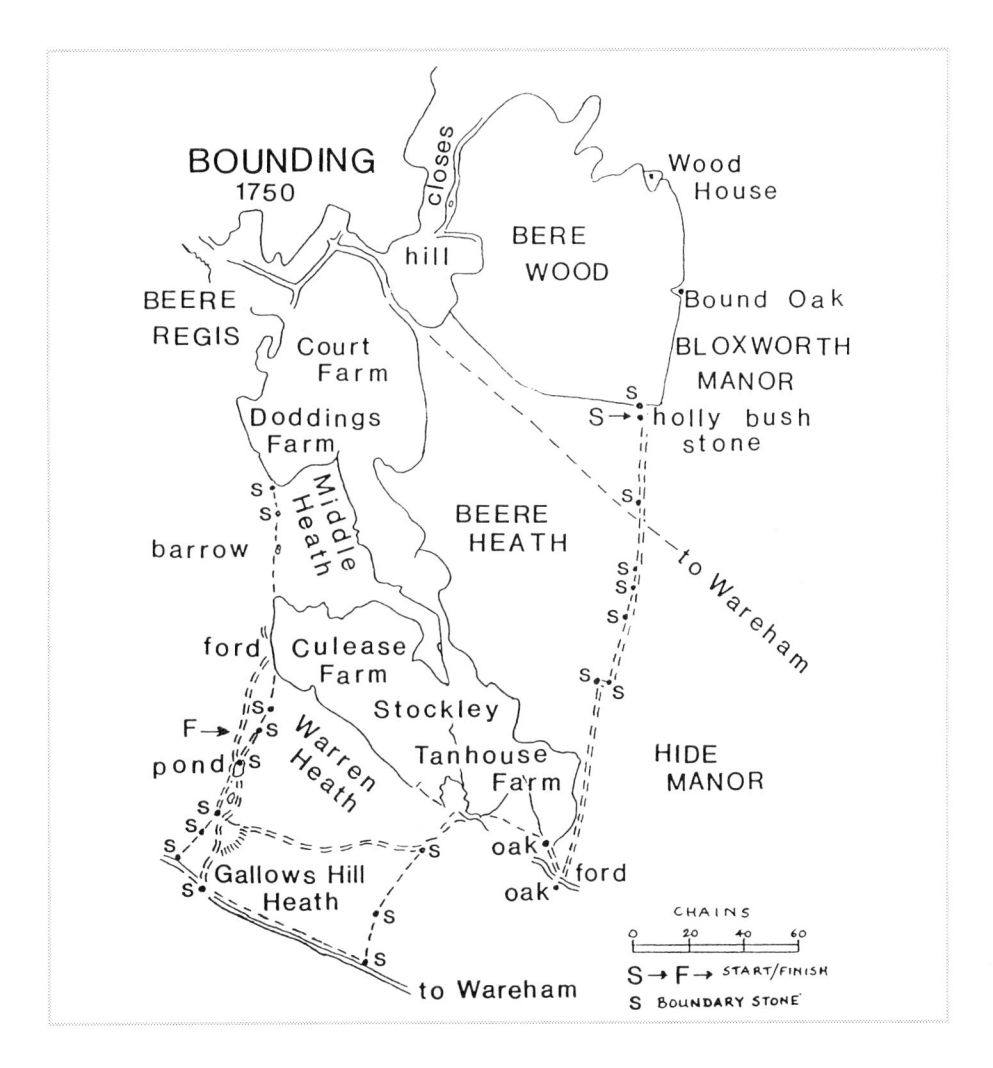

BOUNDING 1750
The map shows the direction taken by 'Beerfolks & bloxworth people' when they met together on June 6th 1750 to beat the parish bounds.

Amongst the local people who were concerned with the maintenance of the site was a man named Gould who was a carpenter. For many years the Goulds had kept a notebook containing an extraordinary variety of information about the site, the Fair, the town of Bere Regis and occasionally about the local gentlefolk. In October 1706 there was a wedding in Bloxworth church between John Goold of Bere Regis and Elizabeth Kennell of Wool and it is possible that the bridegroom was a relative of this unusual family, perhaps a contributor to the notebook. Amongst its pages is a reference to the ancient custom of 'Beating the Bounds' and a detailed description of an occasion in June 1750 when people from both Bere Regis and Bloxworth joined together and "went a bounding".

CHAPTER 6

JOCELYN PICKARD AND FARMING (1751-1800)

Shortly after becoming the owner of the estate, Jocelyn Pickard was involved in a repetition of the dispute over his tenant's grazing rights on common land. The right to take cattle and horses (but not sheep) from the Bloxworth Farms into Bere Wood was an ancient one and whilst there is evidence that it existed as long ago as 1557, it was undoubtedly older in origin. The authority and responsibilities of both the owners of the woods and those who were entitled to use them for grazing had been defined in an Act of Parliament passed in the reign of King Henry VIII. The Act allowed owners to fence off a proportion of the woodland for a period of seven years for the cutting of timber and to allow sufficient time for the newly planted trees to become established but those who held the rights, known as 'common of pasture', were permitted to use the remaining areas. The right of access was unpopular with the owners and, as mentioned earlier, had been the subject of quarrels and litigation in the past. Once again, those concerned were reminded that Bloxworth cattle had been impounded in 1582 and in 1615. However, in 1733 an agreement was signed between Henry Drax who owned the wood and Roger Pinchard, the tenant of Bloxworth Farm. The latter agreed to accept an annual payment of £5 on condition that he avoided using the wood for grazing.[1]

The solution suited both parties at the time but when Jocelyn Pickard became the new owner, he considered that the right of access should be restored. It seems that the Drax family wished to purchase the right for all time but the new owner of Bloxworth was prepared only to lease it for a maximum of twenty-one years at an annual rate of £30. Niggling correspondence and bargaining followed. Jocelyn Pickard mentioned his agreement to the making of a gate between Bere Wood and his Cow Leaze for 'convenience in hunting' and asked that the gate be kept locked except in the season when 'the Gentlemen are pursuing their Diversion' as the 'Country People are making bad use of it' and he was anxious to avoid any claim of 'Right'. He also indicated that the owner was welcome to put up as many gates as were needed between the properties and referred to the many rabbits in Bere Wood which he desired should be destroyed or kept under control as much as possible. It is clear that each side considered that the other was acting unreasonably and that neither intended to give in. Bere Wood had already been closed by the owner to the farmers who were his tenants and it was now proposed that the rights of the Bloxworth Farm should be limited to the comparatively small parts of Bere Wood known as Holming Coppice and Berham Breach. Mr Filliter and Mr Nicholls who were acting as attorneys for the Drax

THE POOR LAW

A Settlement Certificate

To the Church Wardens and Overseers of the Poor of the Parish of All Saints in the Town of Dorchester in the County of Dorset.

We the Church Wardens and Overseers of the Poor of the Parish of Bloxworth in the said County Do hereby certify that we own Edith Gregory Widow, John her Son & Mary her Daughter to be Inhabitants legally settled in our said Parish of Bloxworth And We do hereby promise for ourselves & successors to receive them in our said Parish whenever they shall become chargable. In Witness whereof we the said Church Wardens & Overseers have hereunto respectively set our Hands & Seals this 28th day of January 1755.

Witness	*Jocelyn Pickard*)	*Church Wardens*
Roger Pinchard	*Robert Stickland*)	
	David Abbott)	*Overseers*
	William Bennett)	

* * * * *

The Poor Law was introduced in 1601 to provide public relief for the destitute and one of its main principles was that parishes should be responsible for those who were settled there as defined by the law. The parish registers show that Mary, the daughter of Richard and Edith Gregory, was baptised on September 16th 1753 and that Richard Gregory died and was buried on January 19th 1755. Edith would have become Bloxworth's 'own' by virtue of her marriage to Richard and had probably decided to move to Dorchester following his death.

In 1772, another of the Bloxworth Settlement Certificates was concerned with the case of a young, unmarried girl who was expecting a baby. The Churchwardens and Overseers persuaded two men (one was the father) to enter into a legal agreement that they would pay £50 to the Overseers if there was any demand on the Poor Rates in consequence of 'the birth education and maintenance of the said child ... '.

estate visited Bloxworth in January 1759 to explain and discuss the proposals. Jocelyn Pickard was clearly incensed, particularly by the attitude of one of the lawyers. In a copy of a letter to a friend he wrote indelicately 'Nicholls took a great deal of pains, with a Countenance as demure as an old whore at a stoning ...'. It is not known whether there was an immediate settlement but the business was decided eventually in 1846 by the passing of the Parliamentary Enclosure Act for Bere Regis.

By 1744, the three Bloxworth farms known as Dyetts, the Middle Farm and Zouches had been combined into one farm and Roger Pinchard was appointed as the tenant of this large single farm. To the north of the parish Marsh Farm was outside the Bloxworth estate and the remainder of the parish was either owned by the Church (The Glebe Farm) or was tenanted by ten copyholders and ten leaseholders. They included seven men who had been the backbone of Bloxworth life and were properly described as Yeoman Farmers. Robert Alner had copyhold estates in Piddlehinton and leasehold estates in Bloxworth. He and David Abbott were men of substance and much respected in the community and their names are recorded on one of the bells which still hangs in the church tower. Robert Stickland made bequests amounting to £241 and Matthew Abbott's estate was valued at £233 nearly half of which consisted of 'live stock':

> Four cart horses with harness
> One hackney gelding
> Six milch cows and one calf
> Three 3-year old heifers
> Two 2-year old heifers
> Four yearling heifers
> Three pigs
> One hundred and thirty-two sheep

Amongst Bloxworth's other leading citizens was Thomas Gallop who was a butcher like his brother Benjamin. Thomas was an entrepreneur who acquired interests not only in three small properties in Bloxworth but others in the nearby villages of Morden, Lytchett Minster, Sturminster Marshall and Shapwick. He and his wife Jane, who was better known as Jinny, had three sons and a daughter but Thomas died when the youngest of the children was only six years old. He seems to have had a premonition of his impending death for although he made provision for the properties to be divided between his sons when they reached the age of twenty-one, he also requested that his friends Joseph Manuel and William Fookes should look after the properties during the boys' minority. His daughter, named Sarah, was to receive £200 when she reached the age of twenty-one and Jinny was provided for as long as 'she keeps herself in my name and unmarried' and she continued to manage the Bloxworth properties for some years after her husband's death. The Dean of Sarum appointed Joseph Manuel and William Fookes, together with Robert Burge of Muston and James Kitcat, a Bere Regis victualler, to be the administrators of his will. Unfortunately, the details of Thomas Gallop's property and possesions have been lost and there is no record of what happened to his wife. Sarah Gallop was married in Bloxworth Church in February 1799 at the age of twenty-one.

One of Roger Pinchard's successors as manager of the Home Farm was a man named Samuel Crane who kept a farm diary for fourteen months during 1770-71 which has provided a detailed description of farming practices during the latter part of the Eighteenth Century.[2] Presumably Samuel Crane was appointed by Jocelyn Pickard and no doubt the diary was to enable the owner to keep a careful check on the value and development of his property. In earlier times the country had been farmed by large numbers of tenant farmers, a system which suited the character of the people, both landlord and tenant, but small farms began to be uneconomical and the need for farms to be grouped together in larger units had already begun. As the economic conditions changed, inability to meet bills and pay the rent forced small farmers to accept that their land should be taken over. Sometimes landlords waited until the leaseholds had expired but the prevailing economic conditions led to considerable changes in the structure of village life and a great deal of hardship to those who for generations had managed their own affairs. Those who resisted the changes in other places were to lose their tenancies as a result of the Parliamentary Enclosure Acts but in Bloxworth the changes occurred gradually and there was no need to introduce the measure. In the next door parish of Morden the Act became a Statute in 1769.

Most of the farm lay on chalk land, although to the south, where the Glebe Farm was situated, the ground was of heavy clay. Further south beyond the extensive woodland, there was heath and sandy, stony soil. It was a mixed farm and the principal income came from sheep, wheat and barley but the variety of the work extended to every aspect of farming. Apart from his duties as the manager of the Home Farm, Samuel Crane had responsibilities for the Glebe Farm and the collection of tithes from some of the other Bloxworth farmers. These included wagon loads of wheat, barley and hay but there were also smaller quantities of other crops such as oats, peas, clover and sainfoin, the latter being a type of pea used for animal feed. On two occasions small sums were paid instead of the farm produce and once a large sum of money is mentioned, presumably the tithe for the Home Farm paid in cash rather than in kind:[3]

November 13th 1770 pd to [?] & The Rev Mr Bromfield for the tith in Money & Desbersments £131-18-4

Samuel Crane was also responsible for paying taxes for the estate and there are references to Land Tax, Window Money, Poor Rates and the Hundred Silver.

There were cattle in Bloxworth but dairy farming was much less important in the late eighteenth century than it is today, and the management of the dairy herd on the Home Farm was quite different. The lack of good roads and the inability to move supplies of milk to distant markets meant that the milk was produced only for immediate domestic consumption or for the local production of cheese.

The system of management was for some of the cows to be leased to an individual who made his profit by selling the milk back to the farmers and villagers. Thomas Rodgers looked after the herd in Bloxworth and paid a quarterly rent of £24-0-0 for twenty-four cows from the Home Farm. Apart from selling milk, he was also entitled to sell any of the calves produced by the herd. Each cost £1-2-6d and the sale of calves probably constituted a large proportion of the herdsman's income. Later John Coles of Shitterton took over responsibility for the herd and Samuel Crane sent two carts to Bere Regis to help him move his property:

May 14th 1771 6 Horses with 2 Waggons to Shiterton for John Coles goods

Cheeses made in Bloxworth were sold in various parts of the county and despite the poor quality of the roads were dispatched as far as Weymouth, twenty miles away by modern roads, and to Dorchester, Poole and Blandford. Once, two horses were used to take cheese to 'Deanesleze' where one of the Savage family lived at the time when Bloxworth was sold to the Trenchards.

Only occasionally were the cattle killed for beef but one Wednesday in October, Benjamin Gallop came over from Morden to 'bucher' the bull. Later, 635 lbs of beef was distributed amongst thirteen of the regular farm workers with the largest share going to John Baskem who carried home eighty-one pounds of meat. Smaller shares, each of twenty-four pounds, were allocated to Will Cheek and Ann Durrant. Benjamin Gallop was paid two shillings for slaughtering and cutting up the animal but he had to pay £1-5-0 for the bull's hide. He seems to have been favoured in other ways for on two occasions he was charged half the standard rate for wheat. The best cuts of meat - a 'cheek and sheen' - went to John Davis and Richard Stevens who paid extra for the privilege, the average price being 1d-1½d per lb. Meat was probably a rare luxury and there was undoubtedly great excitement as the huge joints were taken back to the cottages to be salted and preserved, when they would provide an occasional special meal during the winter months.

There were between 900-1000 sheep on the Home Farm which were 'washed' a few days before shearing. The older ewes and eleven rams were dealt with in June but the main flock was sheared over a three-day period in early July. Samuel Gould was in charge of the work and in 1770 received £3-5-4 for 'Waishen & Shearing 986 Sheep'. The 'old yeos' were put to the rams in July and a month later the 'flock yeos' were also put to the 'rames'. During the winter some of the young flock were taken to farmers at Fiddleford and Okeford Fitzpaine for keeping whilst others were sold either direct to individual farmers or at the fairs at Wilton, Shroton and Blandford. Preparation for lambing started in December when the hurdles, made by John Small in August at a cost of £2-11-9 for thirty-two dozen, were distributed to their chosen sites and the 'Yeos' began lambing in early January. The spaying of the new lambs took place later and in May John Short was paid six shillings and six pence for 'Cutten 106 Lambs & Cutten 3 Pegs & Spaying a Bytch'. Feeding the sheep was probably left to the shepherd but in July 1771 sheep and lambs were allowed into the fields to graze on the 'vatches'. Part of the farmland was used for the growing of turnips and it is likely that this was for feeding in the autumn and winter when the sheep would be turned out to eat down the root crop gradually.

Dogs were not always well-behaved and an entry in the diary shows that sheep worrying is an old problem:

July 21st 1771 1 Old yeo killd by John King Dogs

Nevertheless, sheep were profitable and in twelve months the profit on the flock was £240-5-3.

There were a few pigs on the farm but it is likely that most families kept at least one pig in their cottage gardens. In May 1771 there was a need to buy pig feed and a cart with three horses was sent to Wareham to collect forty bushels of 'graines for the Pegs'. It must have been poor quality grain, probably the sweepings from the threshing barn floor, for Samuel Crane paid only 2d a bushel for it. At this time the standard price for a bushel of wheat was approximately 6/9d.

Forestry and hedgecutting were important tasks on the estate. Hedge laying was a skilled business carried out approximately every seven years which ensured that the hedges provided continuous and effective fences. It was comparatively slow work and a man was not expected to exceed a chain (twenty- two yards) in a day's work. Payment was calculated by the goad, a measurement of ten feet of hedge. The work was popular and was normally well paid at the rate of 3d per goad although this might be reduced to as little as a 1d, depending on the work involved:

March 18th 1771 pd John Baskem for Maken 120 Goad of Hedg against Cheepmansfeeld £1-10

Copses in the woodlands produced hazel needed for making hurdles to pen the sheep and the wood for spars used in the thatching of cottages and ricks. This provided the forestry workers with a small addition to their incomes:

August 7th 1771 pd Henery Dewlyn for 2000 of Spars £0-4-0

The woodlands and heath were a source of fuel, rarely in the form of logs, more often as bundles of faggots or furze. Furze burns quickly and was used particularly for baking and also for the preparation of lime at the lime kiln — work which was completed over a period of three days during June or July, involving huge amounts of faggots:

July 8th 1770 pd John Baxhem for Cutten 2250 Fuzfaggots for the Lime Kill £1-2-6

Fuel in the cottages came from areas where the collecting of dead wood was permitted but there was always a shortage. Some of the more prosperous in the community burnt turf (peat) and much of it was carried in wagons belonging to

THE PRICES OF MISCELLANEOUS GOODS
1770 - 1771

Barrel of Tar	12 - 0
Five Rakes	2 - 6
A Lamb Poine	2 - 0
A Hanbarow	6
A Speard	3 - 6
Two Corn Vurks	5 - 0
Six Pare of Harvest Gloves	3 - 0
A Whet Stone for the Sythe	6
Five Pare of Stavel Stones	12 - 6
A Barn Suvell	3 - 0 (a)
Two Pad Locks	2 - 0
Four Quart of Oile (for Harness)	2 - 0
Six Sacks	18 - 0
Talow (21 lbs)	4 - 4
Six Rattraps & a Padlock	6 - 6
Sutt (76 bushels)	1 - 18 - 0
A Buckett for the Weell	4 - 6
Tartwine (6lb)	2 - 3

(a) It should have been a good one. On another occasion a barn shovel was bought for 1/6d.

the Home Farm:

November 3rd 1770 Recd of [Daniel Accort] for the Carrige of 4000 of Terves £0-8-0

August 7th 1771 pd Thos Collens for Cutten 200 of Fuzen & 3000 of Terves £0-5-0

The ashes were used for spreading on fields where the clay was particularly heavy. It was collected from the cottagers who received six pence for each wagon load. Coal was an expensive luxury and, in a twelve month period, it was collected only five times from Poole and once from Wareham:

August 10th 1771 2 Waggons with 8 horses to Waraham ... & Brought 2 Load of Coles from Hide & White ... pd Stephen White & Hide for 40 Bushels of Coles at 19 pence per Bushel £3-3-4

The two main crops were wheat and barley. All the corn was cut, stooked, dried in the sun and stacked by hand using horses and carts. The ricks were carried to the barns gradually throughout the winter and in early summer so that it was not until July 17th 1770 that Samuel Crane was able to record, referring to the 1769 crop, 'Finished Traishen and Wimmen the Wheat'. Seven weeks later, on August 23rd, twenty farm workers began to cut and bind the new wheat crop on two fields and four days later they were able to start 'Maken a Rick'. In a year, the profit on the sale of wheat was just over £197 and this did not include wheat used on the farm, for example, in the Cart Horse Stable.

The barley sowing was in April and was completed during the first week of May. It was weeded during June and cut shortly after the wheat harvest. On September 24th 1770 an entry in the diary reads 'Begun Maken Barly Rick'. Much of the crop was winnowed and sold to John Bundock at Poole but there were a number of other customers, especially Joseph Longman who, apart from buying barley, bought and sold some cattle and provided sacks, malt dust and clover. The annual profit on barley at £186 was only £11 less than the profit on wheat.

Oats were grown on the farm but not in sufficient quantity to meet its needs. Two of the local farmers supplied small amounts but in February 1771 Samuel Crane bought 100 bushels from Farmer Palmeter in Wareham. Other crops included peas and there was a pea rick at New Barn but only a little was sold and the bulk of the crop seems to have been for domestic consumption:

December 24th 1770 2 Bushels of Pease for the Peggs

The writing in the diary is cryptic and factual but on rare occasions Samuel Crane provides more detail than usual. He seems to have particularly enjoyed an experiment with cabbages which were planted on two days in June 1770 in a field named Cutfurze:

June 23rd 1770 Finished planting Cabbages in Cutfurze.
Set, in all, 8 Ridges of 114 in each Ridge, at 2 feet asunder in the Ridge -
Seven of the Ridges are of the Scotch Cabbage, & the other Ridge, against the Turneps, are the common Winter Cabbage - Gave them some Water"

The cabbages were hoed in July and more were planted in another field during 1771 but there is no mention about whether the experiment was as successful as Samuel Crane seems to have hoped. Potatoes were not grown on the farm but were bought on three occasions in 1771, probably to supplement the crop grown in the walled garden of the manor house.

There was a wide variety of activity on the periphery of the farm although most of this was undertaken by individuals in their cottages and cottage gardens.

There were hives of bees:

January 29th 1771 pd R Skinner for 2 Bee Pots £0-1-0

and it was not unknown for some of the more unruly to help themselves to other people's property:

February 3rd 1771 pd for Lock for the Chicken House Doore £0-0-6

There was an elaborate Pigeon Cote at the manor house which was repaired by Will Cooles and four men in June 1770. The large number of pigeons led to the use of a farm cart to remove the 'Piggons Dung' which was used as a fertiliser on one of the fields. Harvesting was thirsty work and there was a tradition that the workers should be rewarded with cider. In 1770, a hogshead of cider was collected in June and another was bought in August. A hogshead contained about 50 gallons:

June 26th 1770 pd John Bundock for 1 Hocksed of Syder £1-11-6

Few farming subjects are not covered in the diary but it is surprising that there is no mention of any reference to the Woodbury Hill Fair. Woodbury Hill is less than half an hour's walk from the centre of the village through Bere Wood. In 1770, the barley harvest had not been completed and there was ploughing elsewhere on the farm when, in September, the Fair was in progress. There is little doubt that the Fair took place in 1770 and that many of those who lived in Bloxworth attended it. Some of the young workers may not have been able to get there until after their work was finished.

A small change took place in farming procedure during 1771 when on March 4th the Home Farm 'Begum Measuearen With the Winchester Bushel'. The 'Winchester bushel' was an attempt at standardisation, for the size of the bushel varied throughout the country and an example of the new standard was kept in Winchester Town Hall. Later, in 1826, it was replaced throughout Great Britain by the Imperial Bushel.

Work on the farm, particularly in the winter, depended on the state of the roads and tracks and the ability to move materials into the fields. Improvement of access to the fields took place in the early summer months, before the harvest, when the ground was fairly dry. The work was usually referred to as 'Way menden' and consisted of filling the existing cart ruts and potholes with flints, gravel and chalk where the route had seriously deteriorated. There was also a need to maintain the approaches and the crossing of streams:

March 9th 1771 1 Waggon Carring ... Planck to the Parsnoge for Bridges

Much of the repair of buildings would have been carried out as a matter of routine. Bricks were obtained from the brick kiln in Morden and one thousand four hundred bricks were delivered to the Parsonage in June 1771.

Although Turnpike roads had been introduced in Dorset in 1752-53, existing

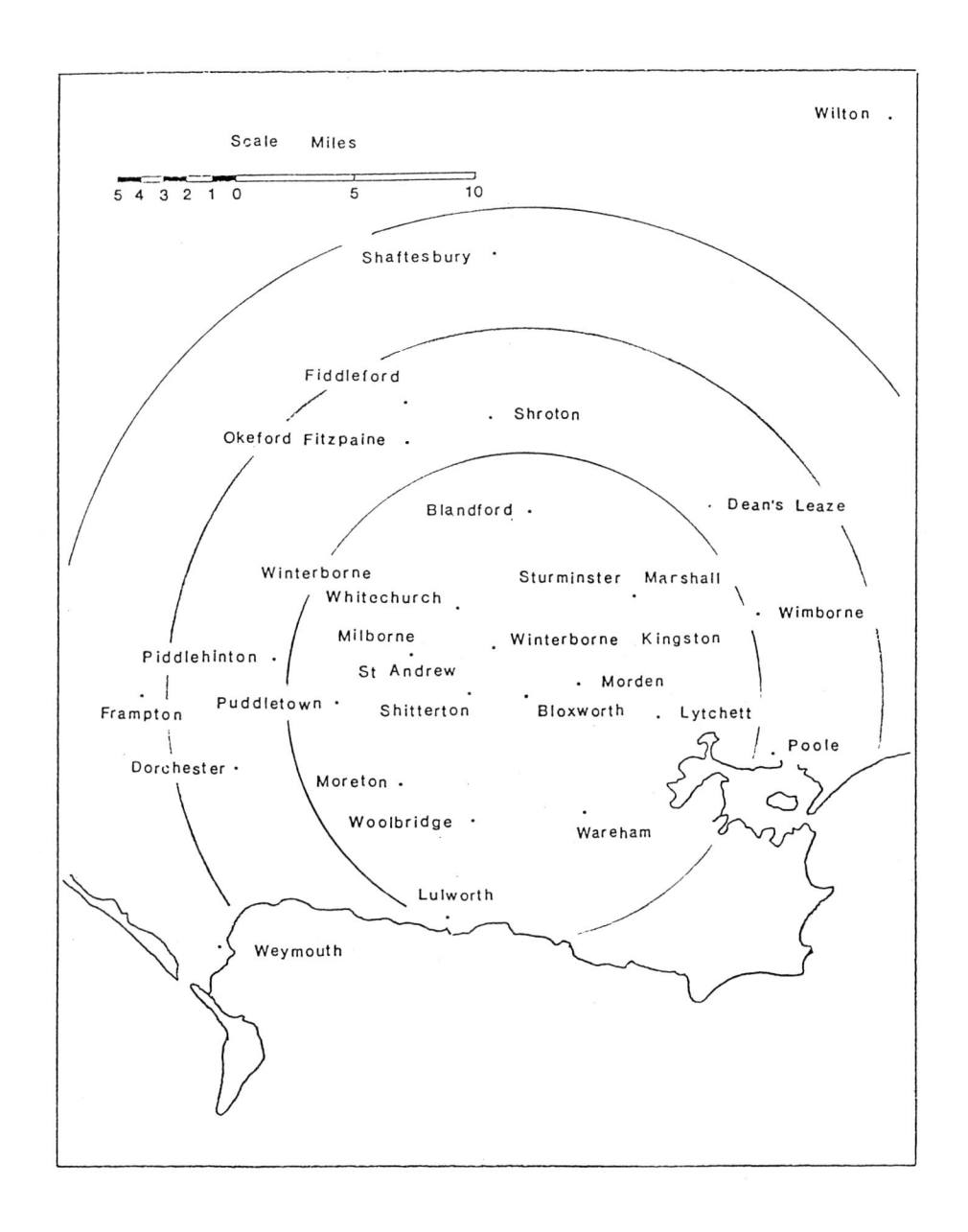

FARMING 1770-1771
Places which were visited by Samuel Crane or other employees of Bloxworth Farm on farming business during 1770-1771. The circles on the map represent distances of ten, fifteen and twenty miles from Bloxworth.

roads, though poor in quality, enabled regular visits to be made to the local towns and goods were delivered to a wide variety of places.[4] Journeys beyond the parish boundary took place on average just over once a week, continuing throughout January and February but becoming less frequent at harvest time. Many of the journeys were undertaken by Samuel Crane on horseback but a large number involved loads, usually of corn. Carts were sent to Poole or Wareham on an average of once a month and these journeys involved Turnpike charges which varied according to the type of load and the regulations at the time. There was only one entrance into Poole, at 'Pool Gate', and the charges varied from 1/1d to 2/5d. The tollgate charges at Wareham were higher but seem to have been the same for all vehicles - the price for each wagon was 1/6d. Loads were also sent to Wimborne (the tollgate was known as Hillbutts) and to Shaftesbury which had the lowest entrance charge (1/1d). There is no mention of tollgate charges at Dorchester or Weymouth in 1770-71.

Samuel Crane frequently mentioned the fairs which took place in the surrounding market towns and larger villages. He was usually at Blandford Fair at four-monthly intervals but in September, when the Woodbury Hill Fair took place, he went to Wilton where he sold eighty sheep and to Shroten (Iwerne Courtney) Fair when he sold '13 Refuze Weather Sheep'. There were fairs at Wimborne, Puddletown, Woolbridge and Dorchester. At Frampton Fair, Samuel Crane bought a bull from Farmer Bunn for five guineas.

* * * * *

The purpose of the Home Farm was to supply the manor house with food and the owner of the estate with income. Very large quantities of corn were sent to the water-mill just outside the parish boundary in Morden and milled barley and wheat were subsequently delivered to the house. In 1770-71, the average monthly delivery of barley was five bushels and of wheat just under three bushels. Deliveries of furze faggots were made and were used to heat the ovens. Peat was sometimes used for fuel and there is a report of three loads of turf being delivered to the house. Oats and hay were regularly sent to the Saddlehorse Stable but the grooms were part of the domestic staff of the manor house and were not the responsibility of the Home Farm manager. A brief note in June 1770 'Two horses and the Chaise to Shitterton' was the only entry referring to work in the manor house stables.

Oats and barley were sent to the Carthorse Stable where at least twelve carthorses were kept for every type of work on the farm - it must have been a fine sight when Samuel Crane borrowed horses from two of the yeoman farmers so that on two consecutive days in June 1771 twenty-one horses were employed helping the farm staff to sow turnips in one of Bloxworth's largest fields. Usually two or three horses were needed to draw a sull [plough] but it was not unusual for larger teams to be used when the wagons were fully loaded. Turfs provided a particularly heavy load and sometimes five horses would be needed to draw each wagon when turf was being moved.

> ## BLOXWORTH CHARITY
>
> In 1786, details of a 'Charitable benefaction to the parish of Bloxworth' was submitted to Parliament:
>
> > *For the poor of Bloxworth parish, in money 5l.*
> > *by whom, when, and how given, is not known; now*
> > *vested in James Jellett, blacksmith, at*
> > *Bloxworth. There is no interest paid at present*
> > *for the 5l. [£5].*
> > *Robert Maurice, minister of Bloxworth, Dorset*
> > *William Fookes, churchwarden.*
> > *Sept. 9, 1786. Sworn before us*
> > > *Anth Chapman*
> > > *Roe King*
>
> The reason for the submission may have been connected with the work of a committee of the House of Commons in 1786 whose task was to investigate the administration of poor relief for it had been discovered that many charities were in danger of becoming lost and many were mismanaged. Charitable bequests appear in a number of old Bloxworth wills.

Samuel Crane must have had his own horse for supervising the work and for the many visits he had to make on business. In February 1771, he bought a horse for £19-19-0 but during the previous year there are two entries in the diary which probably refer to his own horse:

June 14th 1770 brought home Colonel from Grass

October 21st 1770 pd Far Inohem for Keepen of Kernold [Colonel] in the Salt Marsh 4 weeks £0-9-0

* * * * *

Throughout history, descriptions of agriculture and workers have often shown well-fed country folk in their comfortable cottages leading a simple, unskilled, outdoor life. It is a distorted view of the country and far removed from reality. The cottages were 'tied' and families could be evicted without notice. Retention of the home depended on the whole family complying with orders and instructions issued by the owner or his representative and the ability of farm workers to continue to do their jobs. Ill health and old age might become grounds for eviction so that the cottage could be handed over to a fit, younger man. The wattle and daub walls and thatched roofs of the cottages were adequate but there was little furniture, little heating and no interior water supply or sanitation. Each cottage had a large garden providing the occupants with a good supply of fresh vegetables, although the supply had to be spread out over the whole season. Water came from a deep well, often shared by more than one family. The sanitary arrangements, even in the better homes, consisted of wooden huts at the bottom of the gardens.

The Home Farm had three different types of employees. There were eighteen regular full-time farm workers which included three boys and one woman. The annual pay for a man was £15-12-0 and from this would be deducted rent for his cottage of £1-10-0 per year. The second category of workers was eight specialists who provided particular services such as sheep-shearing, hurdle-making and rough carpentry. Casual workers were the last and largest group, numbering thirty-five people, many of them men with their own smallholdings but often the wives and daughters of the regular workers. The specialists usually earned piece rates but the casual labourers were paid at a mixture of day rates and piecework. The standard rate for men was 1/0d per day which was increased to 1/6d during the barley harvest and to 2/0d per day for reaping. Weeding was usually carried out by the women (5d per day) or the girls (4d per day). The casual rate for boys was the same as the weeding rate for girls. The normal rates for piecework were:

Threshing	1½d per bushel
Hedging	2d - 3d per goad (10 feet)
Cutting Furze	1/- per 100 faggots
Mowing	Approximately ½d per acre

Some of the work was unusual. In November 1770, two men were paid ten shillings for 'Shuvlyn the Furryes' in one of the fields. R Stivines received a low rate of only one penny per goad for 'Vylen of 68 Goad of Wood' but in January 1771, B Swyer was paid a guinea for 'a Years Molles Catchen'. During the following February, J Batekem repaired a lighthorn at a cost of six pence and three men were employed in 'Cutten Anthills'. Perhaps the most obscure of the casual work was undertaken by John Smith who received 2/9d for 'the Runners in holm mead'.

* * * * *

In 1780, the Parish of Bloxworth was assessed as part of the '.... granting an Aid to his Said Majesty by a Land Tax, to be raised in Great-Britain'. It was undertaken by two of Bloxworth's senior and most respected citizens, Joseph Manuel and James Jellett, both yeoman farmers. The assessment was based on the value of property and was not necessarily an indication of its size. In addition it included parts of the parish, particularly in the north, which were outside Jocelyn Pickard's Bloxworth estate. In 1780, Marsh Farm was owned by the Reverend John Harbin[5] and a small field in the northern corner of the parish was the property of Lewis Tregonwell of Anderson Manor.

Nearly half of Bloxworth's contribution was paid by Jocelyn Pickard who had already begun to increase the size of the Home Farm by absorbing some of his tenant farms. Another contributor was the Rector, the Reverend Robert Maurice, who was responsible for the payment of the Land Tax on the Glebe Farm. Joseph Manuel, who helped to complete the assessment, was the owner of a small farm in the centre of Bloxworth and was listed among the proprietors. The remainder, thirteen individuals and three joint tenants, were described as holding 'their several Messuages or Tenements under Jocelyn Pickard Esq' and many of these properties were sublet to those who were labelled as 'occupiers'. Two were quite sizeable farms but the remainder were either smallholdings or on poor quality land - possibly both.

By 1790, six of the messuages or tenements, including the two larger farms, had been absorbed into the estate. Jocelyn Pickard died in 1789 and was succeeded by his eldest son, Thomas. The estate was now divided into two, Home Farm and Lower Farm. John Pinder, who managed the Home Farm was also responsible for the Glebe whilst the owner, Thomas Pickard, took over the running of the Lower Farm. His brother, George Pickard, became the Rector of Bloxworth in 1780 and was also Rector of both Warmwell and Poxwell. It was a high point in the Reverend George Pickard's career and it pleased him greatly when he was chosen to preach in Weymouth on October 13th 1799 at a service attended by King George III.

* * * * *

Social life for country gentlefolk was agreeable and attendance at the Races at Blandford was an important social event. The races had been held on the downs at Tarrant Hinton since 1729 and after a decline were revived in 1744 and continued for nearly one hundred years. Thomas Pickard was listed as a Recorder of Blandford in 1784 and there is a report that Mr Pickard attended the Blandford Races in 1786 travelling in a coach with 'a pair of Blacks'. The races[6] lasted for three days and included special features and entertainments - some of them like cudgel-playing and cockfighting were of a very bloodthirsty nature. However, the list of the gentry in 1786 sounds like an extract from a Dorset 'Who's Who' and included the Lords Milton, Shaftesbury, Arundel, Rivers and Digby.

* * * * *

Another assessment was carried out in Bloxworth in 1796, this time unconnected with taxation. The French Revolution began in 1789 and by 1796 there was widespread anxiety about the possibility of a French invasion. Part of the preparations consisted of a survey of the parishes in south Dorset to assess the available stock on the farms in preparation for their possible evacuation to safer areas. The survey was carried out by officers of the Volunteer Dorset Rangers and in his report, Captain Grosvenor of Charborough included the following details for the Parish of Bloxworth:[7]

```
              Bloxworth Farming Return 1796
Number of farmers who made returns        9
Distance from the sea                     10 miles
Distance from the 'safe' area             9 miles
Live Stock           Horses               45
                     Cows                 100
                     Sheep                1180
Dead Stock (acres)   Wheat                100
                     Barley               156
                     Oats                 101
                     Peas                 25
                     Hay                  266
Number of mounted servants
         available to drive stock         1
Number of servants available on foot
         armed with pick, axe and spade   Nil
```

Clearly, Bloxworth was reluctant to provide the manpower to support any withdrawal. As it happened their optimism, or reluctance to become involved, was well-founded but it was not until many years later that Napoleon was defeated at the Battle of Waterloo in 1815 and the danger of invasion had disappeared.

CHAPTER 7
SOCIAL SCENES - AGRICULTURE IN DECLINE (1800-1850)

Thomas Pickard succeeded his father in 1789. He was public-spirited and had been accepted into the highest social circles in Dorset. His memorial in Bloxworth Church mentions his work as Chairman of the Quarter Sessions and adds that he 'passed most of his life at his seat in this parish' although this seems to conflict a little with his appointment as Mayor of Corfe in 1800 and 1802. Certainly he took a keen interest in the development of the farms on the estate but he and his wife had no children and when he died in 1830 the property was inherited by his brother.

George Pickard was seventy-four when he became the owner of the estate. He had been admitted to Holy Orders, married well and for the past fifty years had been the Rector of a small village near Weymouth, where the Trenchards, close relatives of his mother's family, were the patrons and owners. George was a widower when he inherited Bloxworth and his four sons were all well-established. The eldest, Edward, took over the property when his father died in Poxwell in 1840, but not only was he a bachelor but he died only ten years later leaving the estate to his younger brother George, who by that time had, as the result of the terms of an inheritance, changed his name to Pickard-Cambridge.

Young George was brought up in Warmwell and, after completing his education, followed his father's example and entered the church. He was married in 1818 and for a time lived at Corfe Castle where at least one of his fifteen children was born. The parsonage at Corfe was destroyed during the Civil War and a new house was built whilst George was there and the Reverend William Bond was the Rector. This work may have influenced George to rebuild the Rectory at Bloxworth for the construction of the present house was completed between 1822-1825. It is said that George Pickard frequently rode the fourteen miles from Corfe to Bloxworth to see how the building progressed. It is not clear when he moved into his new parsonage for he, too, was Mayor of Corfe Castle on seven occasions during the period 1818-1832 but he was certainly involved in the church services at Bloxworth from 1822 although he did not become Rector until 1850. Of their many children only three were significantly involved in Bloxworth's affairs - Henry and Jocelyn became soldiers and served in the Indian Army whilst their better known younger brother, Octavius, born in 1828, was to become extremely influential both in Bloxworth and elsewhere during the second half of the century.

Between 1800-1830, there was a steady decline in the number of smallholdings as these were gradually absorbed into the two large farms which by 1830 were both controlled by George Mayo, the farm manager. On the outskirts of the estate, only Rebecca Furmage, Samuel James and Thomas Stephens appear in the 1830 Land Tax Assessments listed under the heading 'Messuage or Tenement Holders'. The reduction in the number of smallholders, shortage of work and low farm wages caused great discontent throughout the whole country. The insensitive approach of some landlords and problems created by a few trouble-makers increased the tension. Groups of farm workers became unusually militant with the result that farm ricks were burnt and the newly introduced farm machinery (another cause of the shortage of work) was often damaged. In 1830-31, the troubles in Dorset were centred near Dorchester, at Moreton where the Frampton family were directly concerned and in the Handley and Cranborne area, north-east of Blandford. Fortunately, the disturbances in Dorset were fewer than in other parts of the country due to the quick reaction of the authorities and the presence of a small number of regular cavalry troops. Some of the disturbances occurred in nearby Bere Regis where, as Mary Frampton wrote:

> *On Nov. 22, 1830, the first risings took place in this county .... My brother Frampton harangued the people at Bere Regis and argued with them on the impropriety of their conduct .... This spirited conduct caused him to be very unpopular ....*[1]

At about this time the Dorset Yeomanry was resuscitated and a troop was based at Charborough where it was reported that 'Mr Drax will send over 20 men mounted and armed if required'. This helped to maintain good order although on December 9th 1830 there was news of a rick on fire at Mr Alner's farm near Bere Regis. There was no rioting in Bloxworth and although by 1845 few independent small farms existed - there were still eight men and one women paying rent for very small fields - nevertheless, they maintained some independence and the smallholdings comprised a total of just over thirty-five acres.[2] Although Bloxworth seems to have avoided involvement in the disturbances, this was not so in other parts of Dorset. A total of seventy-one men were arrested on various charges of causing disturbance and whilst fifteen were acquitted, the remainder were found guilty and sentenced to transportation or imprisonment. Moreover, in some places agricultural workers continued to be underpaid. Some tried to improve their lot and eventually this led in 1834 to the arrest and subsequent trial of the Tolpuddle Martyrs.[3]

Curiously it was another trial, unconnected with agricultural disturbances and the Tolpuddle Martyrs, which caused interest in Bloxworth. On March 1st 1834, Sophia Goddard was committed for trial by the Reverend George Pickard, Junior, the magistrate, on evidence provided by Ann Mitchell, John Buxton and others. A brief report of the trial appeared in the March 20th 1834 edition of the weekly newspaper, the *Dorset County Chronicle*:

Sophia Goddard was indicted for feloniously, unlawfully, and maliciously, attempting to suffocate her newly-born female - bastard child at the parish of Bloxworth. - A fellow female servant of the prisoner gave evidence against her in a very clear and intelligent manner, and some points of it were as strong as to leave very little doubt of her guilt; but in the course of the trial some palliating facts were stated by the nurse who attended the prisoner, which left room for the conclusion that the circumstance of the child's being in the vault might possibly have been accidental. The Jury in consequence acquitted her; but the Judge did not omit to remind her that she had lost a woman's most valuable possession - her virtue.

Nothing is known about those who gave evidence against her, or what became of Sophia Goddard. The witnesses might have been employed either at the Rectory or the Manor House and presumably they all left Bloxworth shortly after the trial.

Bloxworth people undoubtedly knew about the agricultural disturbances although they did not participate in them and there is a dubious story about this which may have some basis of truth. Many years later, repairs were being carried out to the roof of the stables at Bloxworth House when two tiles were found inscribed 'Come all you fighten men drew near - J Ings'. Like some modern graffiti, the words suggest a protest which may have originated at the time of the agricultural troubles. Two men might have been able to provide the evidence; both were named John Ings - probably cousins who were born within a year of each other. Both came from nearby Morden and both were married in Bloxworth Church to sisters, Mary and Priscilla, the daughters of William White. Mary was married in 1829 and Priscilla in 1837. John was a gardener and servant and it is likely that he was a member of the staff at Bloxworth House. Priscilla is known to have been living in Bloxworth in 1841 with her two children who had both been baptised in Bloxworth Church. There was a brickyard in Morden during the 1830's and it has been suggested that John Ings (Mary's husband) worked in the brickyard where he made the tiles whilst John Ings (Priscilla's husband) had them placed on the stable roof.

* * * * *

George Pickard Senior lived at Warmwell and was the Rector of the adjacent villages of Warmwell and Poxwell. In the curious way that these matters were arranged, he was also the Rector and Patron of Bloxworth.[4] Obviously, he had been consulted in the plans for the building of the new Rectory and when this was completed he started work on the reorganisation of the Glebe lands which provided the Rector, in addition to the Tithe, with an important source of income. Laws had been passed during the reigns of George III and George IV to enable 'Spiritual Persons to exchange the Parsonage or Glebe Houses or Glebe Lands belonging to their beneficies for others of greater value or more conveniently situated....'. George Pickard Senior obtained the services of a Wimborne surveyor and in September 1830 submitted the plan for approval. The legal process was extremely slow for no doubt the church authorities wished to be sure that nothing untoward should arise from the transaction and there was a need to be certain that the value of the Glebe was increased as a result of the changes. Eventually a huge legal document was prepared which was signed by the parties concerned including Charles Oldfield Bartlett, at one time the Town Clerk of Wareham, who seems to have been appointed to represent the Bishop. The new Glebe was established on July 7th 1832.[5]

Social services continued to be organised at parish level and, though rudimentary, had the advantages that those involved were familiar with the requirements of the needy.[6] Of course, monies paid out had to be raised from those who could afford it and, as described in an earlier chapter, a Poor Rate was fixed at the start of each year. In 1822, William Swyer, the tenant of the Home Farm was assessed at £1-5-6, an apparently small sum, but during 1822 each rate payer had to pay thirty-three Poor Rates and the contribution by William Swyer would have been £42-2-10 - more than one third of the total raised.

The lowest rate of a 1d was paid by James Furmage for 'his Leasehold'. The list was signed by four of Bloxworth's leading citizens and countersigned by two men from outside the parish including Mr JJ Farquharson, who lived on an estate at Langton Long near Blandford and was known principally as a Master of two packs of Foxhounds.[7] Between 1822 and 1835 the annual Poor Rate expenditure varied from £112-£166 and a proportion of this - just over a quarter - went towards the County Rates.

A small number of people (there were four in 1823) received a monthly allowance which was known as the 'monthly establishment' and varied from ten to sixteen shillings. Others were paid different sums to meet more specific needs. Mary Davis was sixty years old when she died in 1824 and was buried on June 15th:

June 16th 1824 Funeral Expenses Mary Davis Coffin 14/-
Shroud etc 5/- Clark 4/6 Lay Out 2/- Total £1-5-6

The money collected from the Poor Rates was used in a variety of ways. It paid for the maintenance of the Poor House in a far corner of the village at Woodlake. In 1825, the roof was repaired using one hundred and twenty bundles of thatch (£1-6-8) together with an unspecified quantity of spars (4/10d). The thatcher was paid 15/2d for completing the work. Repairs were needed again in 1828 when three different men were employed at different times at a total cost of £4-17-9. Fortunately the place ceased to be used as a Poor House by 1845 although sadly this did not mark the end of poverty in the village.

The rates also paid for medical treatment and medicine. Doctor W Nott received £8-11-8 on March 20th 1825 and there is another entry 'To Mr Baskett for medecine 9/10d'. Payments were made for caring for the sick and the dying and for the care of children who became orphans. In 1829 the Fry family were mentioned frequently in the accounts, not only the result of poverty but also the deaths in March of William Fry, aged only forty-five, and young Joseph Fry, aged

A FARM COTTAGE
In 1846, an article appeared in the Illustrated London News commenting on the accommodation and conditions of farm workers in Dorset. The picture here is of a cottage in the neighbouring parish of Morden and was probably similar to many elsewhere. The article described the sketch as 'a charmingly picturesque bit for the painter; though its propped-up walls, and decaying thatched roof, but too closely indicate the privations of the inmates.'

six, in the following May. Occasionally, the entries are less sombre:

> *October 8th 1828 To Wm Burden for 20 leeches usd by Henvil during his illness 8/4.*

At 5d per leech, this seems to have been quite expensive treatment.

The income for the account was not only derived from the rates for a number of entries refer to the Bastardy Account to which fathers of those born outside wedlock were required to contribute. One man paid £4-5-0 in 1830 and £5-14-6 in 1831 but it is not clear whether the increase was the result of revaluation or further misconduct. Entries in the 1832-33 account show that three men were making payments for their children.

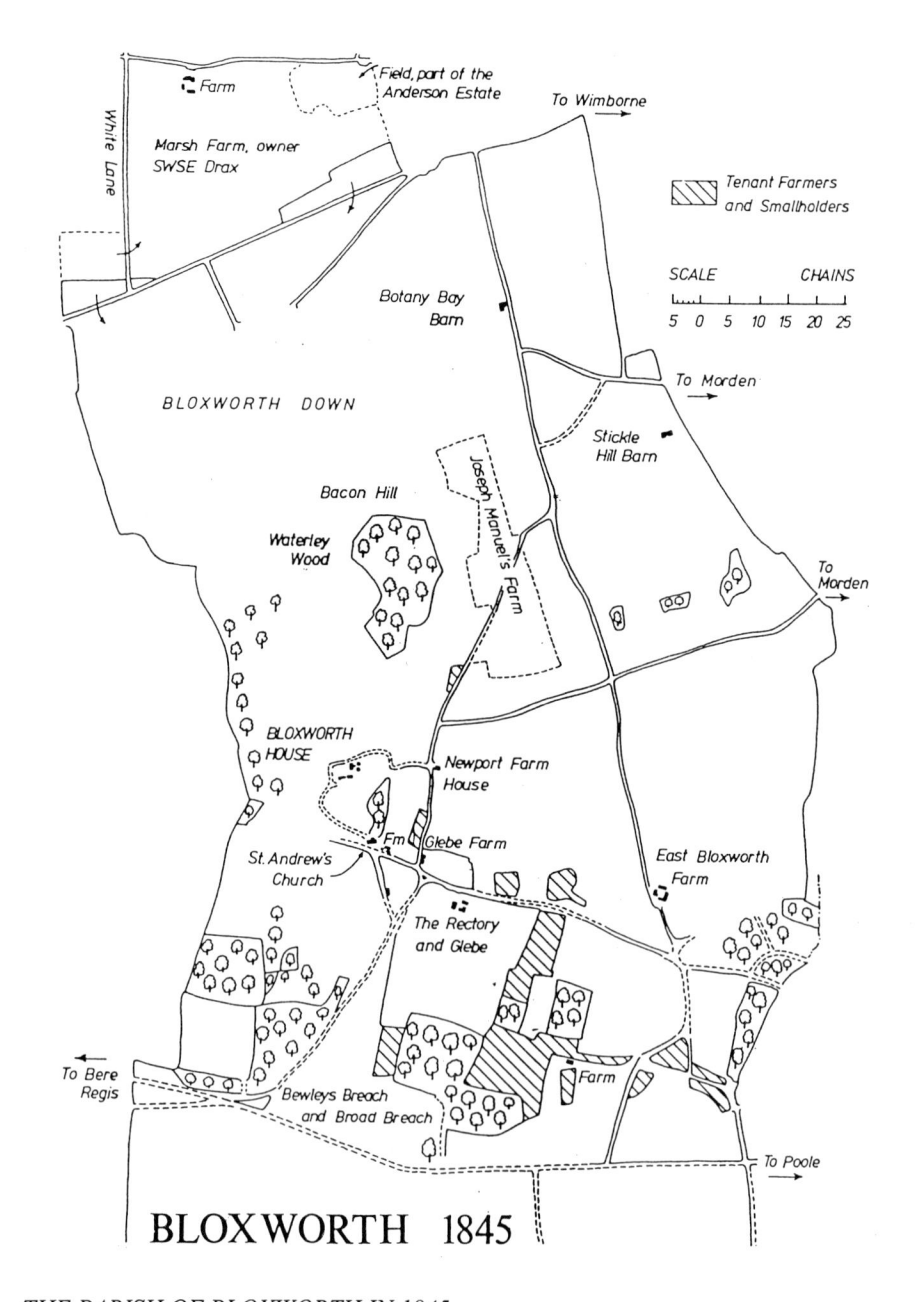

THE PARISH OF BLOXWORTH IN 1845
The map shows the old parish boundaries of the farmland of Bloxworth and is based on the Tithe Map of 1845. The majority of the parish formed part of the Bloxworth Estate but, in the north, Marsh Farm was owned by Mr Drax of Charborough. The Glebe Farm lay in the southern part of the farmland where there were also a number of tenancies and smallholdings. Further south, there was heathland. Map prepared by Alan Graham.

Those responsible for the account were able to pay the rents of those who could not afford them and a series of payments were made in three successive years (1825-27) to Mrs Pickard and were described as 'Houserent'. People from outside the village who were down on their luck were not welcome and the law allowed action to be taken against them. It was quicker and easier to arrange for them to be moved on towards the parish to which they belonged and money from the Poor Rate was used for this purpose on at least one occasion:

January 17th 1825 Relieved a traveller 6/- Car[riage] of Do to Whitchurch inn 5/- Total 11/-

Not surprisingly one of the most popular activities amongst the gentry was fox-hunting. In 1835, Mr RS Surtees, a considerable authority on hunting, visited the area and subsequently wrote an article using his nom-de-plume 'Yorkshireman':

About ten o'clock one night, in the early part of December last, I forget the exact date, I found myself turned out of the Weymouth coach at Blandford, and having transferred myself and my traps into a yellow post-chaise, I set out for Bloxworth House, the hospitable mansion of Col. Lethbridge, for which place I had started some horses a few days previously. After rattling a few miles along the Dorchester road, the line suddenly diverged, up a country lane to the left, and, after passing through divers fields, commons, and opens, and winding about the tortuous byroads, which all countrymen delight to follow, I found myself sitting on an open down, over which the road declined tracking. The post-boy, who got off to open a gate, now came past the window to resume his seat, and I hailed him to ask if he was sure he was right. "O yez, Zur," he said, for he had a touch of Zummerzetzhire twang about him, "it be all right - these be Bloxworth Downs and the House be just over the hill before us; these 'ere white heaps you zee marks the road - they be what we calls Dorzetzhire mileztones".

I looked out of the window on the right, and by the light of the moon, which gleamed dimly through the passing clouds, I saw small heaps of chalk, laid at intervals of five or six yards apart, which, contrasting with the dark sward of the turf, pointed out the line, and guided us over the downs, bringing us ultimately to the door of Bloxworth House, a roomy, old-fashioned, family mansion, the property of Mr. Pickard, situated near Woodbury Hill, the site of a great annual horse fair.

Surtees had come to Dorset to see James Farquharson and he met up with Farquharson's Cattistock hounds at Came Park, near Dorchester. The description of the county continues:

....Of all the countries I have ever been in, Dorsetshire is the most difficult for a stranger to find his way about. Fingerposts there are none; downs, with their 'Dorsetshire milestones', stretch about in all directions, and the cross-roads, over the bleak and barren heaths, are puzzling beyond

description. My line to covert this morning gave me a good insight into the nature of part of the country, and, had I not had a good pilot in Col. Lethbridge, who has lived and hunted in the country for many years, I could never have found my way there at all.

Within the parish the work of maintaining the roads and tracks was the responsibility of two men who in the first half of the century were known as the Surveyors - appointments which were later renamed Waywardens. In 1822-23, the two men estimated that there was more than four and a half miles of highway within the parish. The cost of maintaining the roads was funded by the parish and the details were recorded in the Highway Maintenance books. The income was a charge on principal landowners and their tenants and the majority of the payments were made to men (and sometimes women) for their labour on the roads.

April 26th 1824 Daniel Furmage - 7 weeks on the road in the Parish at the Cross and White Lane.   £2-16-0

June 8th 1824 James Soaper for drawing & screening 20 loads of gravel at 9d per load.   16-8

[Presumably the entry should have read "10d per load"]

There were other expenses too - and some of these include expressions which are no longer in use.

January 7th 1825 Wm Legg: for taking up 163 Lugg of sides of the road on the ridge way at 2d per Lug.   £1-7-2

July 20th 1825 M Lillingstone's bill for making a bunney across the road by Farmer Watts gate.   £2-7-5

September 3rd 1827 Billett for 500 bricks for bunnie across the road £1-2-6

Most of the culverts were made of bricks and were built to withstand the weight of the heaviest farm carts. Work on the road was usually paid at 1/0d or 1/2d per day but exceptional conditions were better rewarded. In February 1855 there was a heavy fall of snow and those who worked on snow-clearing received 1/6d per day.[8]

In 1836 Parliament passed the first of the Tithe Commutation Acts abolishing the payments of tithes in kind and substituting an equivalent Tithe Rent-charge to be paid in cash. To obtain the necessary information, extensive surveys were made and detailed maps were drawn of almost every parish in the whole country. Bloxworth was included in the survey and its map was produced in 1845. It included the names of the owners of both land and buildings and also those who occupied them, the names and exact sizes of the fields, woods and properties and the uses to which they were put.

From 1801, and for each ten year period from that date a census was made of the population of the whole country.[9] In 1841, there were 306 people living in the parish. Most of the adults were agricultural labourers but the numbers included eight farmers, four carpenters, two blacksmiths, two shepherds and two gardeners. The only woodman, James Davis, lived with his wife and five children all under the age of eleven in Bridles Cottage and ten years later there were nine living in this small home.[10] The Reverend George Pickard lived in the Parsonage not far from Bridles Cottage and his name is listed in the census with ten of his children and five living-in servants. His wife must have been away for her name is not on the list. Bloxworth House was occupied by the family of William Bragge who is described as 'Army HP'. He was probably an Army Officer on 'half-pay' though this did not prevent him from keeping a staff of seven including a Governess together with five female and two male servants.

Amongst the Parsonage children was Octavius Pickard, then aged twelve. In 1844, his name appears with two others in long-hand on the bottom of a printed list of pupils at Mr Barnes' School in Dorchester. They were described as 'THREE GENTLEMEN in Military and other courses of Study' and seem to have been treated differently from the forty-two pupils whose names are in print. The Reverend William Barnes (he was ordained whilst he was a schoolmaster in Dorchester between 1835-1862) was an unusual, extremely talented and enlightened teacher with an astonishing range of interests. Many years later the former pupil wrote a lengthy obituary of the Reverend William Barnes in which the school is mentioned:

In 1835 ... Mr. Barnes ... removed to Dorchester and opened a school in Durngate Street, from which a further move was not long after made (1837) into more convenient premises within a door or two of the Dorchester Grammar School, next to the Almshouses, on the east side of South Street. Here for some years his school filled and prospered ... And not only did Mr. Barnes thus simultaneously carry on his school work and private studies, but he found time for extra lessons to pupils desirous of getting on ....

Later in the same article, Octavius wrote:

Every morning during his scholastic life before the regular school work began he gave his scholars a short lecture on some natural history or scientific subject. Each scholar had to take down in writing a proposition, generally embracing one point only, on which the lecture was based. Notes were to be taken upon the lecture, which was always illustrated by objects or experiments, and an examination upon it was subsequently made. I have still in my possession the MS. notes of these lectures during the whole of the two years that I was a pupil of Mr. Barnes.[11]

There is little doubt that the young Octavius was much influenced during the two years he spent at Mr Barnes' School. In 1849 he moved to London to study law for two years but this was as much a failure as his education in Dorchester had been a success. Eventually he was sent to live with a tutor in Somerset in order to study for entrance to a university. It was in 1847 that his father became a beneficiary in the will of a distant cousin, the terms of which required him to incorporate the surname of the cousin with his own. As was mentioned earlier, to meet the requirement the family name was changed to 'Pickard-Cambridge'.[12]

CHAPTER 8
PROGRESS AND PROBLEMS (1850-1900)

Farming continued to provide the main source of work in the village but there was a gradual reduction in the numbers of men and women employed on the land. At one time, the number of agricultural workers was reduced from fifty-three to thirty-eight and the high total in 1871 included children whose tasks on the farms had been omitted in earlier returns. Stephen and Harry Coakes, twins aged 11, were listed as bird 'starvers' and their elder brother Jessie aged 12 was a ploughboy. An average of seven carters cared for the shire horses. It was important work for farmers still depended on well-trained, strong cart horses for the heavy work on the farm in spite of the introduction of modern farm machinery. There was only one dairyman in the whole of the parish but there were seven or eight woodmen to keep the extensive woodlands in good condition. Sheep continued to be important and there were two and sometimes three shepherds to manage the flocks.[1] The sixty or more people directly involved in farming were supported by two carpenters and two blacksmiths. The latter were, of course, involved in the important tasks of keeping the horses well-shod but they were also responsible for the manufacture and repair of many of the implements and fittings on farm tools and farm machinery.

For much of the time up to twenty people were employed in the bigger residences in the parish. Bloxworth House was often let to gentlefolk who usually arrived with their own domestic staff and there were a number of servants in the Rectory, the Lodge and, to a lesser extent, in the houses of the farmers and farm bailiff. A governess, housekeeper, nurse, cooks, housemaids, parlourmaids, a nurserymaid and general domestic servants all formed part of the indoor staff of the more affluent - quite apart from a varying number of laundresses. In 1851 there were three men servants - Sir William Chatterton was the tenant in Bloxworth House with an indoor staff including William Johncock, a House Servant. The Rector had a Footman aged 48 who came from Exeter whilst one of the farmers, Robert Anstey, employed a young fifteen year old boy, George Lovel of Morden, as an indoor servant. There were outdoor staff as well. One or two gamekeepers made sure there were sufficient birds for the shooting parties and there were nearly always four gardeners keeping the grass and flower beds tidy and growing vegetables and soft fruits - Bloxworth House had a sizeable, walled kitchen garden.

In the background were those who tried to make a few pence to help to support their families. Originally the work concentrated on button making and at one time there were thirteen women buttoners who were self-employed, working in their

EARLY HARVESTING
The picture shows the horses and the type of machine used for reaping in the 1870s. The two shire horses 'Prince' and 'Blossom' took part in the film of Hardy's novel, Far From The Madding Crowd. Walter Gale, a former carter, can be seen holding a third horse.

own cottages, but the introduction of machine-made buttons meant that the unfortunate buttoners could not compete financially with the industrially made products. Glove making was introduced but did not last for long but there was a continuing need for a small number of seamstresses or dressmakers.

The level of population between 1841-1861 showed a fall of just under 15% and then steadied to a figure of between 260-270 for the next thirty years. To some extent the high figure resulted from the large number of children between the ages of 0-9 (including an unusually high number of girls) which in 1841 totalled ninety-two. Ten years later, the same group numbered only sixty-four and by 1861 the group had been reduced to twenty-seven. The death of many of the children was a main cause of the decline, fifteen (16%) of the 0-9 year olds failed to reach the age of nine. The total number of deaths was twenty-four but an additional forty-one must have left the village, some to be married but many undoubtedly because of the economic circumstances - that larger, better farms and fewer smallholdings provided less employment than in previous years.[2]

* * * * *

George Pickard Junior was fifty years of age and had been established as the Curate of Bloxworth for more than twenty years when his father died in 1840 and he was appointed as Rector of Warmwell and Poxwell in his place. However, he stayed on in Bloxworth where the Reverend Carrington Ley was the Rector and George was his Curate. For some time churchmen had been involved in the

'THE MADDING CROWD'
Many local people took part as extras in the film. The three members of the cast here are Mrs Fanny Gale, Mrs Lillian Battrick and Mrs Winifred Hunt (later Mrs Middleton).

education of young people, a development from Sunday Schools and the limited teaching of elementary subjects by the parson. The extent to which George Pickard Junior was involved is not clear but there is no doubt that he participated in both the start of formal education and its continuation in the parish. By 1845, one of the semi-detached cottages not far from the church had been set aside and was described in the records as 'School House and Garden', the property of the Curate's elder brother, Edward, who was the owner of the Estate. Mary Baker, a spinster aged forty-nine from Morden, was established as the head teacher by 1851 and was assisted by the twenty-six year old Sarah Henville, the daughter of Walter Henville, one of Bloxworth's carpenters. She and her sister, Elizabeth, became head teachers in turn and were involved in the school for more than twenty years. If numbers are a criterion of excellence, the school soon became a success. From eighteen pupils in 1851, the school increased to sixty-five ten years later and although there was a subsequent decline the high level was restored by 1881.

The school continued with the minimum of outside control until 1863 when the Bishop of Salisbury began inquiries about parish schools. Regularly each year until 1879 questionnaires were sent out seeking information from parsons about the education available in their parishes. George was now in his seventies and there is little doubt that the school was supervised directly by his son, Octavius, who had become his Curate. However, in 1864, the old man filled in the form rather tersely with the explanation:

School is wholly maintained by myself. Boys cease to attend school at 10 or 11. Girls at 11 or 12

Changes took place amongst the village hierarchy as the elderly retired and died and their relations or sons took over. Edward Pickard died in 1850 and left the estate to his nephew Henry, Octavius's elder brother, whilst Octavius became the Rector after their father's death in 1868. Octavius began to think of ways of improving the education facilities and within five years plans were drawn up for a new, purpose-built school on a site provided by the estate. The work was carried out by two builders from Bere Regis, Henry Galton and William Sheppard whilst the contract, which was dated February 14th 1873, named three who were described as the 'employers' - Henry and Octavius Pickard-Cambridge and George Young, Yeoman, the manager of the Bloxworth Farm. The principal conditions in the contract were:

The cost to be £673

The work was to start on March 1st 1873 and was to be completed by September 29th 1873

The Contractor [Henry Galton] would forfeit £2 per week for any delay beyond the completion date

The new school was a considerable improvement on the old thatched house, half of which was used as school rooms and the rest as teachers' living accommodation. Now both the teachers and their pupils were provided with a smart, brick-built building with a slate roof.

The land for the building of the school was given by the estate and the legal document set forth conditions which included instructions not only on the teaching but also the appointment and dismissal of the teachers. The buildings were 'to be for ever hereafter appropriated and used for a school for the education of children and adults, or children only of the labouring, manufacturing and other poorer classes of the Parish of Bloxworth, and for no other purpose'. The school was to be managed by a committee consisting of the Minister and his Curate together with four other persons ...

Provided they contribute at least £1 p.a. each to the funds of the school and are Communicant members of the C of E and possess at least a life-estate or are resident in Bloxworth or an adjoining parish.

The first four men to be appointed were Henry and Jocelyn Pickard-Cambridge together with George Young and William Swyer who were both Churchwardens and Bloxworth's leading farmers.

It is unlikely that the village had its own shop until the late 1840s when William Russell, who had previously been employed as a gardener, began a new career as a grocer, opening a small shop in a thatched cottage just outside the Rectory. By 1855, and possibly earlier, the little shop was also the village Post Office providing a mail service:

> ... *William Russell receiver. Letters through Blandford arrive at ¼ to 9 am; despatched at ¼ past 4 pm. The nearest money order office is at Wareham*[3]

Old William Russell died in 1880 but his family maintained close connections with Bloxworth for many years. Both his father and mother, and also his wife, were all buried in Bloxworth Churchyard. His brother, Daniel Seller Russell made a bequest leaving £200 in his will, part of which was to be used for the maintenance of the family's graves:

> *... and the remainder of the said yearly dividends or income (if any) shall be retained by the said Vicar & Churchwardens and applied by them in the purchase of such books as they may think fit for distribution amongst the day-school Children residing in the Parish of Bloxworth aforesaid whether attending school belonging to the Established Church or Board Schools as prizes for good conduct or proficiency in learning and the following words shall be written or printed in the first page of such books or as near unto as circumstances may require namely 'This book is to (A or B as the case may be) for good conduct or proficiency in learning and is purchased by money left to the Parish of Bloxworth by Daniel Seller Russell a former resident in the said Parish*'[4]

The prizes were first presented to eighteen children on August 21st 1888 but it was almost the end of the Russell family's association with the village. For a time there were two establishments, one a Post Office and the other a Grocer and Draper's shop. By the end of the century the two were amalgamated and the shop was situated in premises opposite the new school.

Octavius was now established at the centre of Bloxworth's affairs. From his private tutor in Somerset, he had moved to Durham University where he obtained a degree and prepared for Holy Orders. In 1859, at the age of thirty, he was ordained as a priest. He had many interests outside the church for he was an outstanding naturalist and a foremost authority on spiders for which he was elected later in his life to be a Fellow of the Royal Society. He was a founder member of the Dorset Natural History and Antiquarian Field Club and was first its Treasurer and later its Vice-President. He wrote articles on a wide variety of subjects associated with his observations of nature. He was a competent artist and an able musician who played the violin well and enjoyed singing. His earliest association with Bloxworth as a priest was in 1860 when he took over as a Curate but in early 1864 he travelled to Europe and Egypt, fell in love following a chance encounter and in 1866 he was married in Oxford to Rose Wallace. Eventually they had a family of five surviving boys - another boy had died in infancy - and

OCTAVIUS PICKARD CAMBRIDGE
Octavius Pickard Cambridge was born in Bloxworth in 1828. He became the Curate in 1860 and remained in the village until his death in 1917. His influence on village life was profound and his reputation as a naturalist extended far beyond the county.

both the parson and his wife lived in the Rectory at Bloxworth until the end of their lives.

Octavius became Rector when his father died in 1868 and in the following year he introduced a church project which he must have been thinking about for some time. Church affairs were discussed at Vestry Meetings which were attended by the two Churchwardens, both leading farmers, two Overseers - the Shopkeeper and the Blacksmith - and four Ratepayers who were leading citizens in the parish. There was unanimous agreement to the Rector's proposal to the putting of '.... a new arch into the East End of the nave of the Church at his own expense'. In fact, the work was much more complicated and involved taking down and rebuilding the whole of the chancel using, where possible, the old materials 'as far as they may be sound and good'. The external dressing was to be of Doulting Stone whilst inside the church the new stone material was described as Corsham Down. Some Purbeck Marble was used to make the step by the Communion Rail whilst the tiles around the altar were manufactured by Maw and Company 'of the value of 15/- a yard'. Devonshire marble columns were provided for the chancel archway and the cost of all the restoration work was to be £545.

Authority was needed from Salisbury for the work to be carried out and plans and a petition were sent off in the approved manner. There was a delay in obtaining approval as a Meeting of the Consistory Court had to be postponed when Bishop Kerr died but within a short time the formal proceedings were completed and by the following summer the work was finished. The service to celebrate the new chancel was attended by eighteen clergymen including, as the Bishop of Salisbury's representative, the Venerable Archdeacon Thomas Sanctuary who 'delivered an eloquent and impressive discourse'. The Chancel had been furnished with gifts from numerous relations and friends - it was a happy occasion and there was every reason to suppose that, as the Archdeacon said at the end of his address, 'God would bless all the ordinances of the Church in that place'. Octavius had arranged a marquee on the lawn of the Rectory to entertain one hundred guests after the service and 'Mrs Drake, an old servant of the family, had been specially engaged to superintend the arrangements, and she discharged her duty with the utmost skill and satisfaction'. There were speeches, of course, starting with one from Octavius who said that his would be short. He proposed the loyal toast:

Looking upon the Queen as head of the country, both in Church and State, he believed that it was only by upholding the union between them that they would all get along comfortably together (Applause)

Another speaker regretted the unavoidable absence of the Bishop and the Archdeacon, replying said that 'if his friend the rector would open his church when convocation was sitting he could hardly expect to be honoured by the presence of the Bishop (Laughter)'. Octavius spoke again, this time at length, in response to the toast to 'the health of their kind Host, Mr Cambridge' and other

---

ADVERTISEMENT

FOR SALE, BY PRIVATE CONTRACT, at the Rectory, Bloxworth, Dorset about 30 Hogsheads of good, sound, CIDER, in Lots of 5 hogsheads, or less if required.
For terms, &c., apply to Mr. H. RICHARDS, Auctioneer, Abbott's Court Farm, or Mr. RUSSEL, Post-office, Bloxworth, Blandford.   [1586

This advertisement appeared in the March 12th 1868 edition of the Dorset County Chronicle and Somerset Gazette shortly after Octavius became Rector.

speeches followed, including, a little later, one by his eldest son, Robert, aged three, who 'stood up to respond on his mamma's behalf'.

It was clearly a triumph for the newly appointed Rector and after all the guests had left:

> *The schoolchildren and villagers were regaled with tea in the rectory grounds. Evening service commenced at six o'clock. The church was crowded.... Mrs Morrison played the harmonium ....* [5]

One of the most loyal villagers was John Skinner. Born in Corfe Castle in about 1796, he must have arrived in Bloxworth early in the 1800s for by 1817 he had been appointed as the Parish Clerk, a position he was to hold for sixty-two years. He and his wife Martha had six children and although in early life John had been an agricultural labourer, later, when he was over seventy, he preferred to be known as a gardener. John Skinner must have known about music and before the introduction of the harmonium it was probably his responsibility to keep the music for the church orchestra. He handed a total of eight carols to Octavius and these formed the basis of what were to become known as the 'Dorset Carols'.[6] The conscientious Parish Clerk was to receive less welcome recognition for a most unlucky accident. For many years the church owned an Hour Glass which in the past had reminded preachers of the passing of time. In a description of the Hour Glass, Octavius wrote:

> *About eight or nine years ago, while the chancel of the church was under restoration, the old Parish Clerk, concerned for the safety of the Hour-Glass, placed it in a chest in which the Church Bible and Prayer Book were kept. Afterwards, forgetting that the Glass was there, he one evening replaced the Bible (weighing about 22lbs.) rather heavily upon it, and with an unfortunate result; the Glass being broken in two at the narrow part. A glass-blower was called in and re-united the parts, but in so doing obliterated the passage for the sand, which has now consequently ceased to run.*[7]

John Skinner died in 1879 whilst still holding the office Parish Clerk and having completed many years of remarkable service to the community.

Although George Pickard-Cambridge had lived in Bloxworth House during the 1860s, for much of the time until Jocelyn moved there in 1884 the house was let to different people who seemed to spend only a few years in the place. In 1875, when Henry was the owner, the tenant was John Brampton Stane whose lease included not only the house but also two cottages which were occupied by the gardener and the gamekeeper. Leases were for a total of seven years but another tenant replaced John Stane before the end of the seven year period. The rent was £200 per year but this did not include 'charges and assessments .... now charged under the Rating Act 1874' which had to be met by the tenant. The rent allowed shooting rights over approximately three thousand acres, including part of West Morden, but there were special provisions preventing the tenant from shooting

CHRISTMAS MUSIC
Some of the music for the morning of Christmas Day 1887 in Bloxworth Church.

rabbits on Bloxworth Farm for the owner reserved the right to trap rabbits 'by means of Hay nets dogs traps and ferretts'. Rooks were a protected species and there was a requirement to shoot the game 'in a fair and a sportsmanlike manner' with the final injunction:

> ....and will leave a reasonable head of game at the end of the said term hereby granted and at least fifty Hen Pheasants in or upon the said Manor or Lordship and Lands

One of the clauses sought access by the owner to one of the rooms in the 'mansion house' which was described as 'the room over the kitchen formerly occupied as a dressing room by the late Reverend Pickard Cambridge deceased'.

* * * * *

At the luncheon party to celebrate the renovation of the Nave, Octavius had spoken of his desire to improve the remainder of the Church. For some years nothing had come of this although mention was made of problems in the church at a Vestry Meeting on March 24th 1874:

> *The Rector called attention to the condition of the pulpit sounding board, which he considered unsafe and requested its removal. He also requested the rearrangement of the seating in the Old Singing Pew so that the scandal and annoyance created by the bad behaviour of boys now sitting there might be obviated and stated his intention to resolve this the arrangement*

INTERIOR OF BLOXWORTH CHURCH
The picture is based on an old photograph of Bloxworth Church which was taken in about 1884 after the rebuilding of the chancel but before the renovation of the nave when the pulpit, reading desk and lectern were moved into new positions and the old box pews were replaced. The text over the arch was taken down in modern times.

> on his own responsibility shortly, unless the matters were to be taken in hand by the Churchwardens ...

Vestry meetings took place each Easter. Until 1894 they were an important element both in the affairs of the church and also for some administration at parish level. They were attended not only by the parson and churchwardens but also by ratepayers and the overseers who were responsible for poor relief. One of the members was appointed as the Waywarden whose responsibility covered the maintenance of roads and access to the village. One of the tasks of the vestry was to choose the churchwardens but where disagreement existed the system was that the Vicar chose one churchwarden and the people another.

Once again an eldest son failed to inherit the estate. Henry Pickard-Cambridge, the owner, had an only son named George but the young man died a year before his father. After Henry's funeral in 1884, the solicitor read his will in Bloxworth House. To the consternation of many he bequeathed the estate, not to his oldest brother but, for a lifetime interest only, to his second brother, Jocelyn, and thereafter to Jocelyn's only daughter. Jocelyn became Lord of the Manor and

BLOXWORTH CHURCH

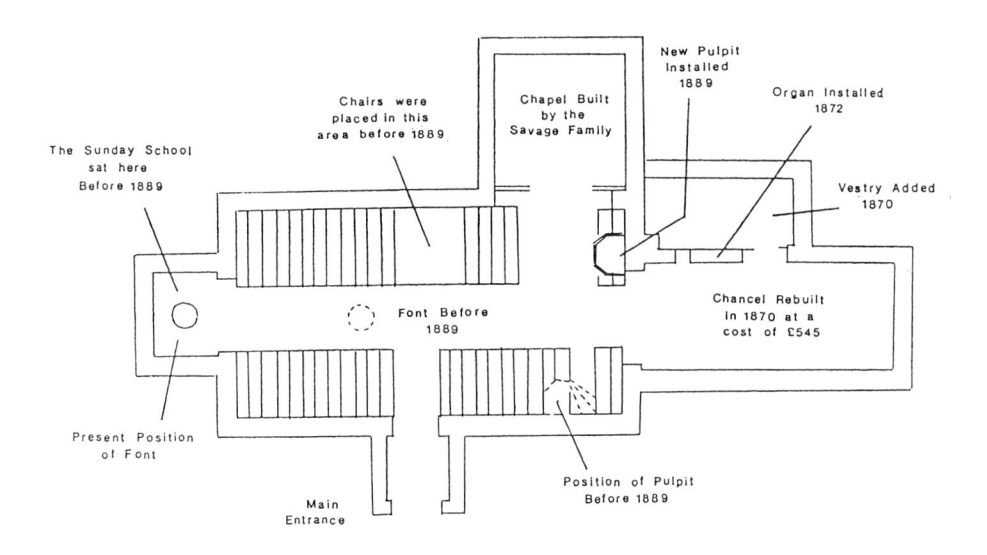

BLOXWORTH CHURCH - THE HISTORICAL MONUMENT
There was probably a church in the village by the end of the 12th century. The square tower and southern walls date from the 14th century but the north wall was reconstructed and the family chapel added by the Savage family in the 17th century. Much work on the interior of the church was carried out in the 1870s and 1880s when the chancel was rebuilt, the box pews replaced and other changes were made - not always with the general agreement of the parishioners.

patron of the living. He moved into Bloxworth House and assumed responsibility as the Squire.[8] Henry had preferred to live in Weymouth and had left the day to day affairs of the village to the Rector, his younger brother, Octavius. Jocelyn had served in the Indian Army and had spent many years abroad and away from Bloxworth. The people of Bloxworth, whether they were the manager of the Home Farm, farmers, tenants or villagers owed allegiance to whoever was in charge and for a time they were faced with a division of loyalty between the Rector and the Lord of the Manor. Both the brothers were strong characters and in retrospect would probably have handled a difficult situation with greater care.

In November 1885, the Rector discovered that the Churchwardens had decided to put a stove into the church for the greater comfort of the congregation but they had not sought his agreement. To forestall them, he locked the Church and declined to allow them entry. The matter was referred to the Bishop in Salisbury who seems to have sided with the Rector but an unseemly row followed at the Vestry Meeting in 1886 and there were no meetings in 1887.

Octavius was determined to carry out improvements to the nave but he had lost the confidence of both his brother Jocelyn and George Young the manager of the Home Farm who were the Churchwardens. Octavius was not deterred and contacted John Bear a builder from Wareham who gave an estimate for the work which involved replacing the box pews with modern seating, removing the pulpit and moving the font to the back of the church. The cost was to be £96 but did not include the construction of a new pulpit. John Bear advised that a separate amount of £30 would be needed for installing a heating system in the nave.

Octavius completed the application for the work to be done and forwarded it to the Bishop in April 1887 without consulting any of his parishioners and although the Bishop arranged for the application to be seen by Jocelyn nothing happened officially until July 10th when Octavius posted the notice giving details of his proposal on the church door. George Young set off to Mr Bear's office in Wareham to find out more about the matter and then wrote to the Deputy Registrar whose signature appeared on the notice suggesting some alterations to the proposed seating plan. Jocelyn wrote on July 15th attacking the way in which the matter had been handled and included the comment 'I beg to bring to your notice that from misrepresentations to the Bishop by the Rector the document is perfectly illegal and that neither of the Church Wardens or any of the parishioners have ever seen the plans referred to'. In a letter to the Bishop on July 16th, Jocelyn made his views clear about his brother '...What I want to show is that the Rector does every thing connected with the church in such an offensive and I am sure illegal manner .... besides which he is leading your Lordship to suppose that everything is being done in a proper straightforward manner'.

Jocelyn's case was weakened by the fact that he had seen the plans in April and knew that Octavius had informed the Bishop that the Rector was willing to meet half the cost of the work. Indeed, Jocelyn had informed Salisbury that he would not contribute to the cost. Meanwhile the Rural Dean was informed and visited Bloxworth to meet those who were opposed to the plan. He seems to have solved the immediate problem for both Jocelyn and George Young wrote withdrawing their objections although the former was clearly the more reluctant '... if my suggestion is not good enough and is overruled then there's an end of the matter'. Octavius was no more tactful when in a letter to the Diocesan Registry at a later stage in the proceedings he included the phrase 'I almost think that he [Jocelyn] does not know what he wishes'.

The faculty enabling the work to be carried out was granted but neither the Rector nor the Lord of the Manor emerged from the proceedings with much credit. The two extremely strong-willed men caused a split in family relations which lasted for many years and divided the village people and their church.

* * * * *

The building of a chapel just beyond the eastern parish boundary may have owed something to the bickering about church matters. There was already a chapel at Whitefield which had been opened in West Morden in 1873 and although the route there from the village was only a farm track, it was not much further from people's homes than the chapel which was built at Woodlake in 1886. It is rumoured that the owner and parson would not allow the chapel to be built and sited within the parish of Bloxworth but that the Drax family had welcomed Congregationalists and Presbyterians in the past and were happy to have another Methodist Chapel within the Morden Parish boundaries. The site was acquired by Mrs Mary Ann Saunders at a cost of £50 and a chapel, carrying the names of Mr and Mrs C Easton on its foundation stone, was completed with all expenses paid, for £145. Worship continued in Bloxworth in separate places but it was not until some years later that the family differences and arguments about Bloxworth Church were forgotten.

THE WEDDING OF MISS PICKARD CAMBRIDGE

A NEWSPAPER ACCOUNT

The return to Bloxworth from their wedding tour of Mr. and Mrs. F. Lane (the bride being the only child of Colonel Jocelyn Pickard Cambridge, of the Lodge; and the bridegroom the second son of General Lane, J.P. of Bexhill, Sussex, was the subject of much enthusiasm on Saturday evening last, when the carriage, containing the happy couple, was met at the entrance to Bloxworth-green by a large concourse of villagers and tenantry who had known the bride all their life. "If you've got Miss Cambridge in there we're just going to pull her up" greeted the coachman from half-a-score of strong fellows as the carriage reached them. The horses were speedily detached from the pole, and, headed by a brass band from Lytchett, playing the 'British Grenadiers', and amid vociferous cheering, the carriage was set in motion, and in a marvellously short space of time the lodge gate was reached. Here loud calls were made for the gallant colonel, who, with a few appropriate words, thanked the villagers for the honour they had done his daughter, and bade them all assemble the following Thursday afternoon at an early hour on the village green with their wives and sweethearts, when he hoped to prove them substantially the pleasure their kindly feeling had afforded him. Mr F. Lane then thanked the crowd again in the name of his bride for their warm-hearted reception, and assured them the day of his return to Bloxworth would live long in his remembrance. Hearty cheers and numerous hurrahs were repeatedly called for and given for the 'young lady' and Mr. Lane, and the crowd dispersed homewards.

The report is from the Dorset County Chronicle and Somerset Gazette on September 23rd 1880. The wedding had taken place in St Michael's Church, Paddington and Mr and Mrs Lane had spent their honeymoon in the Lake District. They left England shortly afterwards on their journey to Ceylon (Sri Lanka) where Mr Lane was a tea planter and where several of their children were born.

CHAPTER 9
THE YEARS OF CHANGE (1900-1945)

Jocelyn died in 1900 and was succeeded by Mary[1] the only daughter of his first marriage. In 1880, she had married Frederick George Alexander Lane and their family consisted of a daughter, who was the eldest, and six sons. Frederick Lane was forty-eight when Jocelyn died. He was born in India, the son of an Army Officer who was a former Deputy-Lieutenant of Sussex. Frederick's standing in the County was high, he became a Justice of the Peace in 1901 and was appointed to be the High Sheriff in 1916. In many ways he was the ideal successor for there was a need to smooth over and forget the earlier family differences.

Frederick and Mary were typical of the age, confident, serious and strict with a sure sense of their responsibilities towards their family, the village and the estate. Once again, it was the owner of the estate who had the most influence on village affairs and to some extent this transfer of authority was helped by the withdrawal of Octavius from public affairs. Octavius was seventy-two at the turn of the century and the onset of old age accompanied by increasingly painful arthritis caused him gradually to reduce his outside commitments, although he continued to work indoors at the Rectory, particularly at his scientific studies. After 1903, he officiated at only three village funerals, two of them for elderly villagers known to him throughout their lives. By 1909, he was unable to continue with his church work and Bloxworth's church was looked after by a curate. The following year his wife died after a long illness but the old man continued to write learned articles on a wide variety of subjects until 1914. Then he began to fail although his death did not occur until 1917.

It is doubtful whether Octavius's work as a village parson was a sufficient challenge for his innumerable talents but it was common practice for parsons to have many different interests and Octavius had plenty of time for his studies. He was loved and admired by his family and it is right that they should have been uncritical of him. There is a passage from the writings of his son Arthur suggesting that he was not always placid or easy to please:

> *He was staunchly loyal to what he regarded as the fundamental principles of Churchmanship and Conservatism, but though he sometimes spoke strongly about those who held other opinions, there was no malice in his words. He often took strong views, and did not give them up easily, but anything that might seem dogmatic in his manner was not more than superficial, and he ordinarily displayed a fine old-world kindliness and courtesy.*[2]

HORSE AND TRAP OUTSIDE THE SHOP
The shop is now a private residence and the bow window no longer forms part of the building. Various suggestions have been made about the identity of the driver but his name has yet to be confirmed.

At the turn of the century there were six farms in the parish - two of them, Marsh Farm in the north and what had become known as Botany Bay Farm in the centre, were not part of the estate. Butlands Farm had been established in the previous century around the main part of the village and it was to increase its size when it absorbed the Home Farm. The Farm took its name from a field adjacent to the seventeenth century dairy house which had been converted into the tenant's farmhouse. As Rector, Octavius had taken over the running of the church's Glebe Farm in the centre of the village in 1883 but the hard work was carried out by the parson's competent dairyman, Harry Danniells. Harry died in 1914 at the age of sixty-nine and was buried in Bloxworth Churchyard where he and his wife, Elizabeth, who had helped him on the farm, share a grave. Later, most of the church lands were absorbed into the neighbouring and larger Butlands Farm.

In the early part of the century Bloxworth or East Farm was the main farm

A VILLAGE SCENE
The thatched cottage on the left of the picture no longer exists. Beyond it, between two brick pillars, is the entrance to the church. The house at the end of the road is the village shop. Sharp eyes may notice that one of the earliest motor cars is parked outside the shop.

and, as the name implies, it lay in the eastern half of the parish. Its tenant lived in a handsome 17th Century house which had been refurbished and added to over the years. Opposite was Steven's (or Stephen's) Farm House, an early 17th Century farm cottage attached to its own farm buildings and the principal house for another of the smaller farms. In 1920, the tenant was George Henry Breen who had once managed the Glebe Farm for Octavius. Now the two farms were to be amalgamated and George had decided that he and his family should start life afresh in Canada. Fifty years later, his son Reginald visited the village to revive the memories which he recalled when he lived in Bloxworth as a young boy. After his return to Canada he wrote a moving account of the visit in the form of a long poem. This is what he wrote about the old farm house:

> *The time is fleeting I soon must go*
> *To visit Old Stevens Farm,*
> *Where I spent so many happy years*
> *Its memory still holds charm.*
> *The old house stands as yesterday*
> *The barn still clings to its side,*
> *Instead of a yard of piglets*
> *A garden of Blossoms showed pride.*

In 1925, a new deed was drawn up between the owner of Bloxworth Farm and the two brothers who were the tenants. It specified that the tenancy was a yearly agreement subject to twelve months notice to quit by either side and that the annual rent would be £115 - approximately one pound sterling per acre per year. The sporting needs of both the landlord and the village were included in the deed. The landlord required access to a field called 'Five Acres' for 'The rearing of Game at the usual Season' and during this period the tenant was not to 'depasture Cattle or Sheep or use the field in any way that may cause the Landlord annoyance'. The villagers' needs were met by the injunction that Field No 151 should be available 'as a football field as heretofore'. A possible agreement about access to water on an adjoining farm was covered in some detail:

> .... the said Tenant Mr Skinner[3] to provide, fix and maintain at his own cost a fence from his boundary to the pond and also a fence dividing the pond into two portions and the said Tenant Mr Skinner shall be entirely responsible for the upkeep of the fences on all sides of this right of way.

The landlord agreed to pay the tithe rent charge, landlord's property tax and the land tax.

The school seems to have been as unpopular with the teachers as it presumably was with the pupils - there were six different head teachers and three different assistant teachers during the eight years from 1903-1910. The solidly built Victorian building with its attached accommodation for the teachers was probably excellent in the summer but was extremely cold in the winter. In the winter of 1917-1918, it was reported that the temperature in the main school-room fell to 44° Fahrenheit and the school managers authorised expenditure on a 'Tortoise Stove' to keep both teachers and their charges somewhat warmer. The remoteness of the village was probably a factor in discouraging teachers to stay and the pay was certainly not a significant inducement. In 1905, the annual salary of the head teacher was £65 and her assistant received only £25. In 1907, the two teachers lived in the school house during the week but set off to their homes on bicycles at weekends. The head teacher lived fourteen miles away in Swanage and her assistant about ten miles distant in Stoborough, on the Swanage side of Wareham.

Octavius continued to attend meetings of the school managers up until 1916 and it was not until the following year that Frederick Lane was appointed as chairman whilst his wife took on the duties of 'Correspondent' - the official title of the person handling the returns and letters between the school and the education authorities. By then both Mr and Mrs Lane had become representatives on the 'Dorset Voluntary Schools Association'.

It is difficult to judge the standard of teaching or the ability of the pupils. After a visit to the school in 1917, one of the Inspectors produced a very adverse report which led to the resignation of both teachers. Pupils were numerate and literate but there were no pretensions that any of the boys and girls were being prepared for higher education. Indeed, the school leaving age remained at 14 until 1930 and it was not until 1948 that a pupil secured a nomination to one of the local Grammar Schools. Former pupils recall Empire Day, always celebrated as a

BLOXWORTH SCHOOL - 1916
Possibly the oldest photograph of the pupils of Bloxworth School. Memories of the comparatively few people who survive and are living in the area are less certain than they were many years ago but names have been added, some tentatively, to thirteen of the children. The lady who can just be made out to the rear of the picture on the left is Mrs MEA Lane who was 'Lord of the Manor'.

special occasion, when the Chairman of the Managers gave an address, no doubt emphasising patriotism and noble qualities. At the end of the formalities, all the children were given an orange and a bun so that on one occasion, a small boy informed an inquisitive visitor that the significance of the celebration was because it was 'bun and orange day'. Only occasionally were matters of discipline discussed by the school managers. In 1903, the complaint by a parent that her son was ill-treated was not upheld and the investigation of a similar complaint, many years later, about the five times caning of a young boy, concluded that the beatings had occured over a period of three and a half years - not excessive punishment in those days.

At the end of 1928, the headmistress resigned and was replaced by Miss Gardiner, another who gave many years of service to the village. She soon became the wife of a builder, Mr L Fortnum, and they lived in the school house. After the Second World War plans were made by the education authorities to close the smaller schools. Every effort was made to retain the Bloxworth school but the numbers were much reduced and in spite of the obvious advantage of keeping some form of education at village level the school closed on July 28th 1960. Mrs Fortnum was presented with a dinner service and a cheque for £10 (paid for by public subscription). Mrs Nellie Gale who had been the school cleaner for more than a decade was given the school's upright piano. The old school building had a happy future - within a short time it was converted into a most successful village club.

BLOXWORTH HOUSE
The picture of Bloxworth House was probably taken during the early 1900s. The lady of the house is feeding pigeons, watched by a pet dog in the foreground. A pony and trap stands waiting by the front entrance of the house.

The village shop was another institution blessed with people providing a remarkable service over many years. It was taken over by the Swyer family just before the turn of the century but Frederick Swyer died in his twenties leaving a young widow with a two-year old daughter. The widow, Ada Kate Swyer, had a sister, Anne Love, who taught in the village school and for a time these two important services were managed by members of the same family. As in most villages, the shop combined the sale of goods with the services of a post office. It was a busy place for few people went to nearby towns for shopping and it was not long before Anne Love gave up her job as a teacher to help her sister full time in the shop. Bloxworth Sub Post Office was originally in the Blandford district but during a reorganisation of the service responsibility for the delivery of mail passed from Blandford to Wareham. Letters in the village were delivered by Frank Squire who started work in 1903 when he received a weekly wage of six or seven shillings a week. He continued to be the village postman until 1948 except for three years during the First World War when he served with the army overseas. Someone estimated that he had walked 165,000 miles delivering letters during his employment with the village Post Office.[4]

Ada eventually retired and the shop was taken over by her daughter who became Mrs Jopling in 1923 when she married a young sailor. In 1939, they sold the shop and moved with their four year old daughter, Hilary, to Weymouth, ending forty years of service to the village by the same family. The shop was and continued to be for many years, a centre of village life. People met, gossiped and

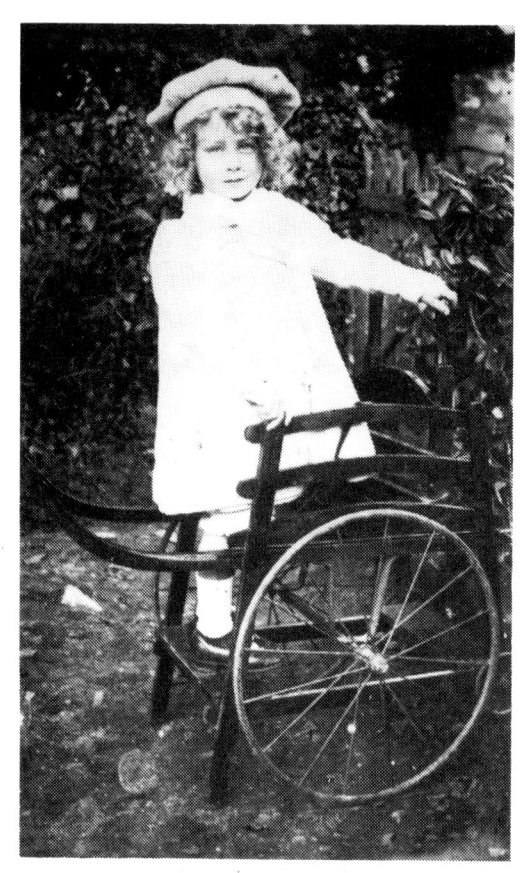

ADA ISABEL SWYER
Ada Swyer was born in Bloxworth in 1897. In 1918-19 she taught in the village school, leaving there to help her mother to run the village shop and Post Office. Eventually she married Leonard Jopling who was serving in the Royal Navy and the family later moved to Weymouth with their young daughter, Hilary. Both Leonard and Ada died in 1979 in Weymouth and their ashes were placed in Bloxworth Churchyard.

passed on information, much of it accurate, often embellished, so that little happened in the village which was not of immediate public knowledge.

Beyond the church was the bakery, run by Tommy Oram and his wife, where the bread was fresh and the baker provided a service for those whose domestic ovens were inadequate to meet the needs on special occasions. Further away, not far from Bloxworth House, was the blacksmith's forge, where old Charles Swyer, father-in-law of Ada Kate at the shop, kept the horses well-shod for their work on the farms. Charles was a Wiltshireman who had lived for a time in the next village until he moved into a cottage opposite the forge. He handed over to another blacksmith, Harry Percy, but neither the shop, nor the bakery, nor the forge exist today - the village has no working horses and the elderly rely on friends and neighbours to take them shopping in places which once seemed far away.

There is a story that soon after the First World War, three young men were walking along the road in the village during normal working hours when they met Mr Lane. He inquired where they were going and on learning that they were on their way to the Dorchester Recruiting Office, told them to return immediately to their place of work and report to their employer, the farmer, Mr Carter. They

A BLOXWORTH FAMILY
The picture, probably taken in about 1910, is of Mr and Mrs Biles with their three children outside their home which was known as "Gardener's Cottage". The cottage, which bore the date '1560' on its wall was, until the 1960s, the oldest house in the village. It has since become derelict.

made as if to carry out this instruction but when Mr Lane was out of sight, they resumed their journey and joined the Army.[5] The village War Memorial bears testimony to those who fought in both World Wars and did not return. Two Elford brothers lost their lives in the 1914-1918 War and another Elford was killed in Burma in the Second World War. Two young members of the Lane family also lost their lives.[6]

After the First World War, Mr and Mrs Lane made an imaginative presentation to the village as a memorial to their two sons who had died during their military service. The gift was a village hall which was built of timber and corrugated iron and at the time provided Bloxworth with excellent facilities. The Memorial Hall,

BLOXWORTH LAND GIRLS
Three girls who were members of the Women's Land Army. The picture was taken in Morden Park, probably in 1919. All the girls were members of the Hunt family.

BLOXWORTH PEOPLE
Mrs Ernest Fancy and her son, Ron.

GLEBE COTTAGES
The history of the three terraced houses in the drawing is not clear. The central part may have been the original house which was later extended to form a pair of terraced houses. Certainly, the house on the right is a later addition. The roof was raised a number of years ago to conform to housing regulations and the interiors have been extensively modernised. The houses are now used as holiday accommodation and for visitors. The drawing is by Mr Fred Fancy of Sandford.

as it was known, was to be used for meetings, concerts, dances and whist drives but it was primarily 'to be used as a reading room for all male inhabitants of 15 years of age and upwards'. The rules which were dated December 20th 1921 were signed by Mr and Mrs Lane and provide an interesting reflection on the standards of conduct and behaviour in the 1920s. The Hall was to be open after normal working hours, on Sunday afternoons and on Sunday evenings after Evensong. No intoxicating liquor, bad language, disorderly conduct or gambling for money was allowed but newspapers were permitted. The level of subscriptions was to be arranged by the Committee which consisted of the President (Mr Lane), a Vice-President (the Rector) and seven members who were nominated initially by the President. One member was required to be in the Hall each evening to be responsible for good behaviour and to ensure that 'the lamps and stove were out'. The Hall was a great success though it seems likely that the rule on gambling may not always have been strictly observed.

In 1927, the Hall was used to entertain members of the Dorset Natural History and Archaeological Society who visited Bloxworth.[7]

THE MEET AT BLOXWORTH
The pack and one of the huntsmen are gathered on the Common at the start of the Meet. Jack and Walter Gale are on the left of the group of villagers who have come to see the horses and riders. The thatched cottage to the rear of the group was once known as 'The Laurels' but was later renamed 'The Old Corn Store' - a reference to its earlier use as a barn.

> *From Bloxworth House the visitors went into the village and had tea in the roomy village hall, which Mr and Mrs Lane have built and presented to Bloxworth as a memorial to their two sons killed in the war - Jocelyn Henry Cambridge Lane (Coldstream Guards) and Walter George Cambridge Lane (Royal Artillery). Their portraits are hanging here, and also portraits of the King and Queen which Lieut.-Commander Herbert Lane, R.N. (another son), recovered from the officer's mess of the cruiser Southampton, which fought at Jutland.*

The Memorial Hall replaced earlier reading rooms which had been at Glebe Farm and Bridles Cottage. It continued to be a centre of village life until 1960 when the school was closed and the school and Memorial Hall became incorporated into the Village Club. Thereafter the old timber building with its corrugated iron roof was used infrequently and became increasingly derelict. It was dismantled in 1992.

Before the introduction of harmoniums and organs into churches, groups of musicians played at the services. At Christmas it was the custom, then as now, for groups of carol singers to tour around the houses in villages. In the previous century, the Parish Clerk, John Skinner, organised the carol singing and the eight carols which he gave to Octavius formed the nucleus of a collection which was sung each Christmas, firstly in the Rectory, later in the church and later still in

SUN BONNETS
In July 1928 an article appeared in The Queen which described the making of six different types of sun bonnets in Bloxworth. It was written by Mary Pickard-Cambridge who was the daughter of Doctor and Mrs FD Lys of Bere Regis and the second wife of Jocelyn Pickard-Cambridge. She was much respected for her work in the village and survived for more than forty years after her husband's death. In May, 1928 The Queen published an article by her on 'Hand-Made Buttons'. The picture is an example of one of the bonnets known as the 'Bloxworth'.

" BLOXWORTH "

the Memorial Hall. The Rector and his relations were particularly fond of music and one of them, William Adair Pickard-Cambridge, was an exceptionally gifted and knowledgeable musician who had many contacts amongst choirs and orchestras both inside and outside the county. By now the collection exceeded 'some hundreds of carols' and Willie Pickard-Cambridge prepared the best of them for publication. The book *A Collection of Dorset Carols* was published in 1926 and more than sixty years later the same collection provides the basis for a carol service each year in Bloxworth Church.[8]

In 1913, the craft of bonnet making was introduced into the village to provide work and pocket-money for women who for one reason or another could not leave their homes to go out to work. There were six different 'Dorset' models and all were hand-made in gingham material of every variety, shade and colour - the prices varying from three shillings for the simpler styles to seven shillings and nine pence for more complicated bonnets. In 1928, a description of the bonnets appeared in a magazine article. Two of the bonnets had 'Bloxworth' names:

The so-called 'Bloxworth' shape has cane in front and cord further back and is made in delightful old-world prints, the dark plum-colour, which was the original 'lilac print', being particularly attractive.

The second bonnet was much easier to make:

Woodlake is one of the simplest shapes and has so little work in it that it is priced from 3/-. It was the only kind still being made in the village in 1913 when the Bloxworth Industry began

The scheme seems to have been a great success for by 1928 considerably more than four thousand sun-bonnets had been made and orders for them had been received from all parts of the world.[9]

There was a continuing need to help those who were in financial difficulties or in poor health as extracts from the Alms Book - 'Expenditure on sick and needy Parishioners' - makes clear. Some of the entries in 1912 indicate part of the problem.

80 dinners at 4d each	£1-6-8
3 pints of brandy (at 2/4 a pint)	7-0
2 bottles of stout	6
4 bottles of Bovril (at 1/9)	7-0

Fred Skinner was paid £1 for three journeys with patients to Bournemouth Hospital and the fund made donations to two people towards the cost of their glasses. The sum of £2-10-0 was allocated to providing coal for three parishioners and a similar amount was given to four others including William Burden who received 2/6 for 'organ Blowing'.

* * * * *

In 1921, the daughter of the much respected John Biles, head gardener at Bloxworth House, married Walter Gale. Two years later their only daughter, Margaret, was born. Walter and Fanny moved into the semi-detached cottage which had been the old school house and which was to be their home for the rest of their married life. The cottage was owned by Mrs Lane and in 1932 the Gales signed an agreement which had been prepared by Mr Lane. The terms which were straightforward are shown on the next page. Mrs Gale and her sister-in-law, Mrs Nellie Gale, shared the semi-detached property which came to be known as Fir Tree Cottages. At a later date, both families became owners of the property.

Between 1917, when Octavius died, and the outbreak of the Second World War, three parsons succeeded each other and lived in the Rectory but from 1939 and throughout the war, the parson and his family occupied the small thatched cottage just outside the Rectory which once had been the village shop. Soon the village would have to share a parson with others - a situation which would have been unthinkable at the turn of the century.

The Bloxworth Cricket Club was in existence in 1904 and the following year Mr Young was thanked 'for the use of the ground' although the need for him to provide the facility was probably well established. The cost of maintaining the

> ## A TENANCY AGREEMENT
>
> This is an example of an agreement between the owner of the estate and one of the tenants. The house (No 1 Fir Tree Cottages) was part of the former school and was eventually bought by the tenants when the estate was sold. The copy of the agreement was lent by Mrs Fanny Gale. Her sister-in-law lived in the other half of the cottage.
>
> Terms of letting: -
> In the Parish of Bloxworth,
> In the County of Dorset, the property of Mrs M.E.A. Lane.
>
> Tenancy from the 10th November 1932
> Subject to four weeks notice to quit on either side.
>
> Rent
> Three shillings per week, payable every four weeks, together with Rates payable to overseer. To keep the garden in good husbandlike order keeping and leaving it, in good heart and condition and free from noxious weeds. Hedges, drains and fences to be kept in good order. When necessary, the interior of the cottage to be colour washed, or white washed, the Landlord providing the material, the Tenant the labour. No nails are to be driven into the walls of rooms, Picture rails have been provided, to which Pictures may be hung.
>
> Chimneys are to be swept regularly, so as to avoid smoky ceilings - and risk of fire.
>
> If the Soakaway pits are clogged, they must be opened and the water drained off. The Tenant is responsible for all locks and keys and to replace them if lost.
> The Tenant not to permit, on the said cottage garden, any waste or drainage, or do anything which may be, or become a nuisance; nor to under let any part of the same without the Landlord's consent in writing.
> I agree to let the above Cottage and Garden on the foregoing terms.
>
> date 10/11/1932 signed "FGA Lane".

Club was small by today's standards - three cricket balls could be bought for ten shillings in 1913 and free teas were provided for home matches. In 1921, the Club was invited to join the Wareham and District League but the decision to do so was deferred for a year. The price of cricket gear had increased so that a bat now cost £1-5-0 and a decent match ball was 15/-. To cover the gentle inflation of the time, subscriptions were increased in 1922 and adults (over 16) now had to pay 3/- whilst those under sixteen became members for 1/-.

The most successful season was in 1933 when the Club won the District

League. A photograph of the 1933 cricket team included the Secretary, John Biles, the Parson, the Reverend Leopold Hewetson Landman, and the umpire, Frank Fancy. There are cynics who allege that Frank played a significant part in the team's success and the comment is usually accompanied by a wink and a chuckle. Cricket continued to be played until war broke out.

After the war the team was revived and in February 1948 a brief report in the local paper refers to a fund-raising Cricket Whist Drive. In 1947, it was revealed that the assets of the Club stood at £1-3-0 but the state of the cricket field had deteriorated. The post-war minutes included the following observation:

> *The condition of the pitch was next discussed. On account of expense, it was agreed to cut & roll the present surface, and endeavour to get it into condition before the winter. Stakes and barbed wire were to enclose the pitch where needed, and volunteers to do the rolling. These arrangements were left in the hands of the Captain [Mr H Gale]*[10]

The matches had been played on a field near Bloxworth House but the need to have access to the farm dairy meant that a new concrete road was sited across the field. It was referred to by Reg Breen in his poem:

> *Slowly my footsteps carried me back*
> *A sadness deep in my heart,*
> *As I gazed on the lonely cricket pitch*
> *That a road had torn apart ...*

The owner of the estate and her family were keen supporters of the Cricket and Football teams and courtesy was observed when decisions were taken at the club's meetings. Mr GH Breen of Stephen's Farm 'kindly lent' the football ground and in 1919 the estate provided the goal-posts. In 1920, the Football Club minutes recorded:

> *...a hearty vote of thanks [was] given to Capt Ernest Lane for the assistance he gave in starting the Club & the great interest he has always taken in it.*

Ernest Lane continued to be helpful and a year later he allowed matches to be played in 'the Park - So as to have the advantage of Shelter, a dryer ground & use of the Pavillion'. It was not expensive to run the Football Club and the membership subscription was only a shilling. Footballs cost 19/- and the groundsman was rewarded with two shillings for marking out the pitch for home matches. The urge to win matches was strong and there was sometimes a need to seek players from elsewhere. In September 1924 the general meeting accepted a proposal:

> *... that the Capt & Hon Scy [Arthur and Frank Carter] be empowered to play 2 men, non resident in Bloxworth, but on the undertaking that they become members, & that preference be shown to resident members of the Bloxworth Football Club*

Percy	Fred	Frank	Frank	Walter	Jack		John
Gale	Biles	Carter	Skinner	Gale	Lewis		Biles
(1)							

	Arthur	Arthur	Joe	?	Percy
	Carter	Short	Cooper	Saunders	Selby
			(2)		(3)

THE BLOXWORTH FOOTBALL TEAM
One of the fields in what is now known as Manor Farm was reserved for football but later on the matches were played in the park. Not all the young men stayed in the village and Percy Gale (1) left Bloxworth to live in the USA. A limited number of players were allowed from outside the village and Joe Cooper (2) came from Morden and Percy Selby (3) lived at Morden Mills Farm. The photograph was taken in the early 1930s.

* * * * *

The chapel at Woodlake continued to provide services and comfort to those who were drawn to Methodism. Memories of those who were involved and details of the events are often conflicting. Some say that Fred White from Sherford was a preacher (he also played cricket for Bloxworth). Israel Davis of Blackheath Farm was a preacher whose father, Edwin, was once a tenant of Butlands Farm. Amongst these worthy men was the serious and slightly austere Frederick Skinner who in June 1933 completed fifty-six years as a local preacher and received a certificate from the 'Connexial Local Preacher's Committee ..... with very cordial congratulations on so splendid a record of service for Methodism and for the Kingdom of God'. Three years later, on November 15th 1936, he was returning to his house on foot after preaching at the evening service. Suddenly he felt unwell and fell to the ground. In a few minutes he was dead. Friends and relations carried him home on a gate and four days later he was buried in Bloxworth Churchyard.

| John Biles (Sec) | Eddie Sawyer | Fred Sawyer | Donald Rolls | Norman Burr (Morden) | Rev Leo Landman | Harold Rolls | Reginald Fancy | Arthur Carter | Frank Fancy (umpire) |

| | Bert Tizzard (Tolpuddle) | Walter Gale | Arthur Short | Harold Snook (Morden) | Fred White (Morden) | |

BLOXWORTH CRICKET TEAM - 1933

The village had a thriving cricket team between the two World Wars. Its chief success was in 1933 when the team were winners of the Wareham and District League. It was a significant effort for so small a village to win this competition, although four of the prominent players were from other villages. The photograph is by James Bridie of Wareham.

CRICKET - BLOXWORTH v BERE REGIS

A Close Run Thing

The match was played at Bloxworth on July 2nd 1921. The first innings provided an exciting and close contest which ended in a tie.

BERE REGIS

W Bagby	Bowled	A Short	1
A Barnes	Bowled	A Short	1
F Lys	Run Out		11
R Jesty	Caught Masters	A Short	0
E Griffen	Bowled	A Short	5
G Hewitt	Caught Breen	A Short	6
S Hewitt	Bowled	R Cosh	11
E Day	Not Out		9
C Hewett	Stumped Fancy	H Day	2
L Barnes	Bowled	H Day	0
B Boyte	Bowled	R Cosh	4
		Extras	4
		Total	54

BLOXWORTH

A Short	C & Bowled	G Hewett	5
H Day	Bowled	G Hewett	4
R Cosh	Bowled	G Hewett	10
F Fancy	Bowled	S Hewett	7
W Masters	Bowled	G Hewett	7
G Breen	Bowled	G Hewett	6
R Fancy	C & Bowled	S Hewett	4
W Gale	Bowled	G Hewett	6
J Lewis	Bowled	S Hewett	0
E Langrish	Run Out		1
S Gale	Not Out		0
		Extras	4
		Total	54

* * * * *

A Short took five wickets for Bloxworth but this was surpassed by G Hewett of Bere Regis who took six wickets. In their second innings, Bere Regis scored thirty-five but the match was drawn for Bloxworth had scored only twenty-one for five wickets at the end of the day.

BLOXWORTH HOME GUARD 1943
The Bloxworth Platoon, led by its commander, 2/Lt J. Gale, is marching past the front entrance of Bloxworth House where the salute is being taken by the High Sheriff of Dorset Mr EFC Lane.
Wags in the village allege that invasion was avoided when the existence of this formidable force became general knowledge.

    The Second World War affected the whole community. A German plane dropped its bombs in the nearby woods early in the war causing craters and damage to the trees. A mock airfield was built on the farmland. A Home Guard section was formed under Second Lieutenant Jack Gale who was better known for his skill as a gamekeeper and forester. The Old Rectory was painted in camouflage colours and became the Air Raid Precaution Post - the stretcher, stirrup pump and splints remained in the house for many years after the war. At least one dogfight took place in the Bloxworth skies and was witnessed by those who were working in the fields. Members of the village were in the forces or worked in the explosives factory at Holton Heath. Some did not survive the war.

FORESTRY WORK
For many years the woods on the estate provided plenty of work although the introduction of mechanical equipment and modern forestry techniques resulted in a reduction in the number of employees on all types of woodland. The picture, taken in the early 1950s, shows Mr Jack Bowles briefing Mr W Birch, the Head Forester. The other forestry workers in the picture are, from left to right, Frank Fancy, Stanley Vowles and Sidney Gale.

Frederick Lane died in 1940 and his wife survived him by only eight months. Both were in their eighties. Two men, Reginald Cuff and Harold Elford, were killed in action in Burma whilst in Bloxworth, Douglas Browning aged 20, died under the tractor which he had been driving whilst working in the fields.

The estate was inherited by Ernest Lane. He was interested in village matters and was extremely popular. It is said that he was anxious to avoid coming upon any of his workers who might be resting (or idling) and to ensure this, he carried a whistle which he blew at intervals to give warning of his approach. He was the last of the true eccentrics to be involved in the running of Bloxworth's affairs. He and his wife had no children and when he died, he left the estate to a nephew. It was the end of the family's ownership of the village. Social changes, the mechanisation of farming, the need for fewer agricultural workers and the reduction in domestic staff all produced problems. Some years later, the estate was sold.

REFERENCES AND NOTES

Abbreviations

DNHAS   Dorset Natural History and Archaeological Society Proceedings.
Hutchins   *History of the County of Dorset* (3rd Edition).
RCHM   Royal Commission on Historical Monuments Inventory for Dorset.

Introduction

1. There is an Iron Age fort at Woolsbarrow in the southern part of the parish.
2. The Romans occupied Britain from AD 43-410.
3. The description 'In King Edward's time....' is taken from Hutchins Volume IV Page 21. See also Hutchins Volume I Page 180. A 'quarenten' is an ancient lineal or square measure containing 40 poles, a furlong or a rood. Here, the size of the pasture seems to have been approximately one square mile.
4. A plaque was placed in Winterborne Kingston Church after the death of George Strangways in 1569.

Chapter One

1. The name 'Strodes Landes' refers to a former tenant. There is another reminder of the Strode family on the road between Bere Regis and Wareham where the road crosses a stream over what is known as 'Strouds Bridge'. Some farms in Bloxworth were occasionally referred to as 'Zouche's', another tenant. In a presentment of 1576 'Charles Zouche gent' was accused of failing to attend church services.
2. The first Bible in English was introduced in 1535.
3. An extract from the *Return of Church Goods made by the Dorset Commissioners of Edward VI* (1552) mentions two chalices of silver and, as was normal, the Church was allowed to keep the second one - 'To the Church's use there is appointed the worst Chalice'. The assessment was made when Sir Edmonde Dorsett was the parson in Bloxworth. See also *Church Plate of Dorset* by JE Nightingale (1889).
4. 'Christian' occurs as a woman's name from the end of the 12th Century. The words of the will have been transcribed into modern English spelling.
5. The name 'Jone' is the phonetic spelling of the modern 'Joan'. The list of property made after a person's death is known as a Probate Inventory.
6. The Parson was responsible for repairs to the Chancel and for buildings on the Glebe Farm. The parishioners met the cost of repairs to the Nave.

Chapter Two

1. Anne Welstead died on January 25th 1640. In those days the calendar year started on March 25th and ended on March 24th of the following year. If the modern system had been in use the date would have been January 25th 1641.

2. The word 'hamme' could mean an enclosure. It is a word like 'parcel' which meant a small area of ground of a size known to local people. The hayward was the village official responsible for fences and enclosures and he would have known the local interpretation of 'hamme'. 'Common of pasture' describes grazing rights.

3. The details are from 'Dorset Suits' - an extract of legal depositions compiled by Francis John Pope. A copy of the work, in fourteen volumes, is held in the library of the Dorset County Museum.

4. The Burial Register for Bloxworth begins in 1579 but does not include any reference to William Dyett. The name 'Dyett' has survived until modern times as there is a field of this name in the parish and houses in the centre of the village are called 'Dyetts Cottages'.

5. Copyholders were tenants of the Lord of the Manor and their rights were established by the 'Court Baron'. Their tenancy was recorded in a copy of the court rolls and they attended meetings of the court.

6. The fair at Woodbury Hill was one of the biggest in the whole country. There is a further description of the fair in Chapter 5.

7. The Overseers of the Poor were elected members of the village who were responsible for providing help and assistance to those who were in need.

Chapter Three

1. The details are contained in the book *Dorset Standing Committee 1646-1650* by CH Mayo (1902).

2. The soldiers concerned were Anthony Combes who served as a Corporal under James Dewey from June 14th 1644 until April 4th 1645 and Joseph Underwood, a private soldier, who was in the Troop from September 22nd 1644 until February 7th 1645.

3. The other members of the commission were Sir Anthony Ashley Cooper and Mr James Baker (a Sequestrator, sometime Mayor of Shaftesbury and later a Member of Parliament). Ashley Cooper was a competent soldier and a man of exceptional talent. He was sufficiently highly regarded that, in spite of his Parliamentary associations, he attained high office after the Restoration of the Monarchy. Eventually he became the Earl of Shaftesbury.

4. The story is curious for there is no obvious connection between James Dewey and the Bankes family who were Royalists. John Bankes purchased Corfe Castle in 1635.

5. The incident is described in the book *Sufferings of the Clergy* by Walker (1714) and also in *The Great Civil War in Dorset 1642-1660* by AR Bayley (1910).

6. The story of the 'excellent, drum-beating parson' is taken from a 1635 report *Survey of Western Counties* which is quoted in Hutchins Volume I Page 120.

7. From the book *Sufferings of the Clergy* by Walker (1714) quoted in Hutchins Volume I Page 120.

Chapter Four

1. The Hearth Tax lists give the names of those involved, the number of hearths and, in some cases, the number of hearths which were no longer in use because they were 'decayed' (unusable) or 'walled' (bricked up). A summary of the 1673 return for 'Bloxworth and Abbots Court' indicates that in thirty-four houses there were ninety-nine hearths. Three persons were exempted from tax.

2. Some of the paintings of the shields were destroyed when other memorials were added. An article on the Armorials of the Savage Family by James Salter is contained in DNHAS Volume X (1889) on Pages 153-160.

3. See RCHM Volume II Part 1 Page 26 and an article by the Reverend OP Cambridge in DNHAS Volume III (1879) Pages 34-35 which describes the Hour Glass in Bloxworth Church.

4. The Savage family owned a number of properties outside Bloxworth including Tarrant Monkton.

Chapter Five

1. See Hutchins Volume III Pages 329-330. Sir John Trenchard was married to Phillipa Speke who came from Somerset.

2. The information is from FJ Pope's *Dorset Suits* which is described in Note 3 to Chapter 2. The claims by Dame Phillipp in 1705 included payment for 'Building the pound in Bloxworth'. Captain Pitt may have been related to a well-known family of Blandford Saint Mary.

3. It is not clear how Jocelyn Pickard and his wife Henrietta came to own the Bloxworth estate. Some say that Jocelyn bought the property at the time of their marriage. Other reports suggest that the estate formed part of a wedding settlement.

4. 'Essoignes' is a corruption of a French word and means 'matters to attend to'. It was also used to record non-attendance.

5. The original document dated 1714 giving advice to the parson on the collection of tithes is held in the Wiltshire Record Office.

6. The dates of the Wills quoted in the paragraph are as follows:

William Alner	1712	Elizabeth Alner	1733
Henry Reeves	1717	Elizabeth Strangeman	1739
John Hucker	1719	Benjamin Watts	1742
Joseph Jefferies	1728	David Abbott	1748

Many of the early Bloxworth Wills and other historical material are held in the Wiltshire County Record Office.

7. The Poor House is sometimes described as the 'Parish House' in the village records. One of the cottages in the south east corner of the village on the 1845 Tithe Map is described as 'Part of old Poor House and garden'. The map is held in the Dorset County Record Office.

8. A record of 'Disbursements' by the Overseers of the Poor was begun in 1659. It has been suggested that the payment for vermin was both a subsidy for the poor besides being a system for reducing what was probably a comparatively minor nuisance.

9. Concern about the wool trade led to the introduction of a law requiring shrouds to be made of woollen material. Entries in the Burial Register at the time were certified by the Rector, John Savage, 'All those were buried in Woolen'.

10. References to the Fairs on Woodbury Hill appear in many local histories, amongst them an article by the Reverend OP Cambridge in DNHAS Volume VII Pages 93-98. A more recent account is contained in *The Book of Bere Regis* by FP Pitfield published by the Dorset Publishing Company in 1978.

Chapter Six

1. The earlier reference to the rights of common of pasture in Bere Wood is in Chapter 2.

2. This type of Farm Diary may also be referred to as a 'Waste Book'. The record kept by Samuel Crane is held in the Dorset County Record Office.

3. The payment of tithes by cash rather than in kind is sometimes referred to as a 'modus'.

4. Further details are contained in *The Old Roads of Dorset* by Ronald Good (1966). The Shaftesbury and Sherborne Trust provided the first of the Dorset Turnpike roads.

5. Marsh Farm was subsequently sold to Evelyn Shirley and later to RCD Grosvenor Esq when it became part of the Charborough Estate.

6. Some details of the Blandford Races are included in Hutchins Volume I. An interesting article on the Races appeared in the July 1986 edition of the magazine *Dorset Life*.

7. A copy of the complete survey of south Dorset farms in 1796 is contained in an article 'Agriculture in Dorset during the Napoleonic Wars' by WE Minchinton published in DNHAS Volume 77 (1955) Pages 162-173.

Chapter Seven

1. The extract from Mary Frampton's description of disturbances in Bere Regis in 1830 is quoted in DNHAS Volume LII (1930) Pages 90-93.

2. The information about the Messuage and Tenement holders has been extracted from the 1845 Tithe Map and Apportionment held in the Dorset County Record Office.

3. The full story of the Tolpuddle Martyrs is told in *The Martyrs of Tolpuddle* published by the TUC in 1934.

4. George Pickard is not shown in Hutchins as the Patron of the living, only as the Rector.

5. The original document describing the alterations to the Glebe Lands was known as an 'Indenture'.

6. The details which follow are taken from The Poor Book 1823-1836 which is held in the Dorset County Record Office.

7. A biography of JJ Farquharson, *The Meynell of the West* by AH Higginson (Collins) 1936 is mostly about fox hunting but it also contains references to Bloxworth and some interesting information about the Dorset Agriculture Society. There is a fine portrait of Mr Farquharson in the Dorset County Museum.

8. A bunney(ie) is a brick arch or wooden bridge. Here, it probably means a culvert. A 'lug' was a measurement equivalent to a pole (5½ yards). The accounts of the Surveyors, which are in two volumes, are held in the Dorset County Record Office.

9. In order to maintain privacy, the details contained in the census returns are not released until one hundred years have passed. The first census was in 1801 but it was not until 1841 that the census returns every ten years contained personal information.

10. The standard of housing in Dorset at the time was poor and an article on cottages in the county appeared in one of the 1846 editions of the *Illustrated London News*. DNHAS Volume 86 (1964) Pages 186-202 contains an interesting article 'Dorset Cottages' by Barbara Kerr.

11. The full text of the obituary of the Reverend William Barnes written by Octavius Pickard-Cambridge is contained in DNHAS Volume VIII (1887) Pages xv-xxvii.

12. An account of the life of Octavius Pickard-Cambridge is included in the book *Victorian Country Parsons* by Brenda Colloms (Constable) 1977. See also Note 2 to Chapter 9.

Chapter Eight

1. The film *Far From the Madding Crowd*, Thomas Hardy's story of the farmer,

Bathsheba Everdene and her shepherd, Gabriel Oak, was filmed largely in Bloxworth.

2. The level of population in the village fell from 306 in 1841 to to 262 in 1861. The comments in the text are based on figures taken from the census returns:

		Male	Female	Total
1841	Group aged 0-9	42	50	92
1851	Group now aged 10-19	29	35	64
1861	Group now aged 20-29	11	16	27

3. The postal information is from Kelly's Directory 1855.

4. The stained glass window on the south side of the nave in the village church is dedicated to Daniel Seller Russell and his wife, Charlotte.

5. The description of the service and the party afterwards is from a lengthy and interesting report in the *Dorset Chronicle and Somerset Gazette* dated July 21st 1870. Other details can be found in *Victorian Stone Carvings in Dorset Churches 1856-1880* by Joan Brocklebank (The Dovecote Press) 1979. Miss Brocklebank also wrote a piece 'The Angels of Bloxworth' for the 1978 Dorset Carol Service in Bloxworth Church. See also Note 8 to Chapter 9.

6. Details of the 'Dorset Carol Service' are given in Chapter 9.

7. The description of the damage to the Church Hour Glass is from an article by the Reverend OP Cambridge in DNAS Volume III (1879) Pages 34-35.

8. In 1886, Jocelyn obtained an estimate from Howard & Sons of Berners Street, London for the installation of new parquet flooring for the Drawing Room and Library in Bloxworth House. The estimate for the work came to £39-13-4 which included oak parquet flooring at 1/4d per square foot and an estimated charge of under £5 for 'Mens railway fare and lodgings and Carriage'.

Chapter Nine

1. Henry left the estate to his brother, Jocelyn, for the period of his life and specified that Mary Ellen Adeline Lane (nee Pickard-Cambridge) - Jocelyn's daughter - should eventually inherit the property.

2. There are a number of books and articles describing Octavius Pickard-Cambridge and the excellence and diversity of his work. Brenda Colloms in her book *Victorian Country Parsons* devotes a chapter (and photographs) to him. His son, Arthur, wrote an obituary published in DNHAS Volume XXXVIII (1917) Pages xli-lii. He also wrote *Memoir of the Reverend Octavius Pickard-Cambridge MA FRS* published privately in 1918.

3. Frederick Skinner was the tenant of Butland's Farm for over twenty years.

4. According to Post Office records Ada Swyer was appointed Sub-Postmistress on November 11th 1899 at an annual salary of £32-10-0. Frank Squire, aged 17, was appointed Allowance Deliverer on May 27th 1904. His weekly pay

of 4/9d required him to work for 1 hour 35 minutes each day and for 1 hour 15 minutes on Sundays. Fortunately, he was able to supplement his wages with other work. He died in December 1959 aged seventy-two. It is thought that he suffered a heart attack and fell into an open fire.

5. The men concerned were Ernest Fancy, Alfred Gale and Harry Hunt who went to the Dorchester Recruiting Office and volunteered for the Royal Artillery (information provided by Mrs Fanny Gale and Mrs Nellie Gale).

6. The names on the War Memorial are:

    1914-1918

    | Cpl H Durant | Serg HP Elford | Pte EB Elford |
    | Pte WR Hunt | 2/Lt Jocelyn HC Lane | Gunr Walter GC Lane |

    1939-1945

    | Pte RA Cuff | Pte HB Elford |

7. Members of the Society visited the Hall and a number of villages on this occasion. The details are recorded in DNHAS Volume XLIX (1928) Pages xlvii-xlix.

8. The first edition of the *Dorset Carols* with a preface by WA Pickard-Cambridge was printed by the London firm of AW Ridley & Co in 1926.

9. The information about the Bloxworth bonnets has been taken from an article in *The Queen* dated July 18th 1928.

10. The information is from a Bloxworth Cricket Club Minute Book.